Book of
Singlets
and
Light Covers

By Carol Balogh

One Printers Way
Altona, MB R0G 0B0
Canada

www.friesenpress.com

Copyright © 2023 by Carol Balogh
First Edition — 2023

Photographer, Cara Rochford, Bijou Bee Photography

All rights reserved.

No part of this publication may be reproduced in any form, or by any means, electronic or mechanical, including photocopying, recording, or any information browsing, storage, or retrieval system, without permission in writing from FriesenPress.

ISBN
978-1-03-916035-4 (Hardcover)
978-1-03-916034-7 (Paperback)
978-1-03-916036-1 (eBook)

1. CRAFTS & HOBBIES, NEEDLEWORK, KNITTING

Distributed to the trade by The Ingram Book Company

To Mom and Grandma,
for without your creative inspiration
I would have never fallen in love.

Table of Contents

Singlets 1
Pom Cami 3
Silk Linen Singlet 9
Hemp Sorbet Singlet 15
Beaded Loop Shell 21
Silk Merino Beaded Shell 27
Camel / Silk / Alpaca / Merino Singlet .. 33
Soliloquy Lace Tee 39
Lovely Locks Shell 45
Alpaca Lace Singlet 51
Buttoned Peplum Shell 57

Light Cover Ups 63
Runner's Sleeveless Kanga 65
Hemp Lace Beachcomber 71
Beaded Hemp Ruana 77
Summer Breeze Vest –Version 3 83
Neo 91
In the Garden Pullover 97
Solstice Cable Leaf Kimono 103
Leaf 111
Cozy Cabled Cardi 117
Round We Go Cardi 125
Yarn Sources 131
Knitting Techniques 133
Acknowledgments 137

Index 139

Introduction

Two years ago, I embarked on a journey to create 20 inspiring designs. It was time to take my design ideas percolating for the last 10 years and build a collection to share with you. Singlets & Light Covers is the result, each design carefully crafted and hand knit by me, pattern captured, written for multiple sizes and presented here with beautiful photos by Bijou Bee Photography.

As you know, we have great weather here in Canada for warm and wonderful sweaters, but this is not the case for warmer climates. I wanted to find designs that would appeal to most regions of the world. Singlets (tank tops or shells) are extremely versatile. Wear alone or layer up with a wrap or cover. Singlets also give you the ability to transition easily from day to evening wear.

In this book you will find I work with many Canadian yarns e.g., 100% wool, alpaca, blends of both, mohair/wool, linen and hemp fibres. Each have great characteristics to create luxury at the skin. It always impresses me that I can find my yarn locally and invite you to seek out local farms that produce their own yarns. Investing in locally sourced natural fibres means we are investing in our renewable future.

Singlets are a great opportunity to explore knitwear construction on a small scale. You will learn how to shape a shell, create armholes and necklines as well as finish them flawlessly. It may be a challenge at first, but really you can only have so many shawls. How about a lovely singlet to go under that shawl? Singlets are generally 3-4 skeins depending on the size, so the investment is smaller given the current cost of yarns.

This book is also an opportunity to explore and add to your knitting skills. To this end, you will find a selection of my favorite knitting techniques I used in the patterns to help you along this journey.

I have been knitting and showing my designs at shows for over 10 years, and I am so grateful for the wonderful feedback I receive. This propels me forward. It is knowing that I have something to inspire you to create for your own – be it the exact pattern or as a jumping off point for your own design. I hope you will find a treasured few in this collection that inspired you once again to pick up those needles. Happy Knitting.

Carol

Designer for Nature's Knit-ch

Singlets

3   9   15   21   27

33   39   45   51   57

Pom Cami

This cami is named for its lovely colour – pomegranate. I wanted to find a pattern that would showcase this luxury 100% hemp yarn and bring elegance to the piece. The Gazebo lace pattern fit the bill. Wear this cami for an evening out with a black lace skirt or top it with a blazer for everyday chic styling.

Challenge Level	INTERMEDIATE
Finished Size	S (M, L, XL, 2X) Bust: 33 (36, 42, 43 ¼, 46 ¾)" (83.8 [91.4, 106.7, 109.9, 118.7])cm Hip: 34 (38, 44, 45, 48)" (86.4 [96.5, 111.8, 114.3, 121.9])cm
Yarn	4 (4, 5, 5, 6) – allhemp6 lux, dk weight, 100g-130m / 143yds, Hemp for Knitting, Nelson, BC, CANADA.
Needles & Notions	4mm (6 US) 14" (35.6 cm) needles; stitch holder; tapestry needle.
Gauge	22 sts and 24 rows in 4" (10cm) using Gazebo Lace Pattern (Row 17 & 18 repeat) with 4mm (6 US) needles.
Care Instructions	Hand wash with a gentle wash product. Lie flat, block and air dry.

Stitches used

M1 – make one

S1 – slip one

Sk2p – slip 1, knit 2 together, pass slipped stitch over k2tog.

Tbl – through the back loop

Bobble (MB): [P1, k1, p1] in next stitch, [turn, k1, p1, k1] twice, pass 2nd and 3rd stitches over 1st stitch.

Gazebo Lace (multiple of 10 sts + 1)

source: p.81 Nicki Epstein's Knitting on the Edge, 2004.

Set up Row (WS): *P5, MB, p4; repeat from *, end last rep p5.
Row 1: K1, *yo, k3, Sk2p, k3, yo, k1; rep from * to end.
Row 2: Purl.
Row 3: P1, *k1, yo, k2, Sk2p, k2, yo, k1, p1; rep from * to end.
Row 4 and 6: *K1, p9; rep from *, end k1.
Row 7: P1, *k3, yo, Sk2p, yo, k3, p1; rep from * to end.
Row 8: Purl.
Rows 9-16: Repeat Rows 1-8.
Row 17: K1, *k3, yo, Sk2p, yo, k4, rep from * to end.
Row 18: Purl.
Repeat rows 17 and 18 until desired.

INSTRUCTIONS

Front

Using long tail cast on method and size 4mm (6 US) needles, cast on 93 (103, 113, 123, 133) sts. Note: Pattern includes 2 selvage stitches; slip the first stitch of every row and knit the last stitch of every row.

Next row: Complete set up row for Gazebo Lace Pattern.

RS row: Start Row 1 of Gazebo Lace pattern or chart. Work to row 18 to complete lace pattern. Continue to repeat Row 17 and Row 18 of pattern until work measures 4" (10.2 cm) from beginning before starting body shaping.

Body shaping: Reduce 1 st at each end of the row 2 (4, 4, 5, 6) times as follows:

For size S every 22 rows, Size M every 12 rows, and Sizes L-2X every 10 rows. Work in pattern without decrease until work measures 11 ½ (12, 12 ½, 13, 14)" (29.2 [30.5, 31.8, 33, 35.6]) cm from beginning.

Next row: Increase 1 st at each end of the row 91 (97, 105, 115, 123) sts. Work in pattern without increases until work measures 13 ½ (14, 14 ½, 15, 16)" (34.3 [35.6, 36.8, 38.1, 40.6]) cm from beginning before shaping armholes and neck edge.

Armhole and neck edge shaping Divide stitches to complete front shaping as follows: Count 46 (49, 53, 58, 62) sts, place remaining 45 (48, 52, 57, 61) sts on a holder. Work a 2 st decrease over the next 2 rows as follows:

Row 1: S1, k2, k2tog, work in pattern to last 5 sts, ssk, k3.

Row 2: S1, k2, purl to last 5 sts, k3.

When 22 (24, 24, 30, 30) sts remain on the needle, work a 4 st decrease over the next two rows as follows:

Row 1: S1, k2, k2tog, work in pattern to last 5 sts, ssk, k3.

Row 2: S1, k2, p2tog, work in pattern to last 5 sts, p2tog tbl, k3.

Work until 6 sts remain. Cast off the stitches.

Complete shaping with the second set of stitches on the holder. Join yarn and m1 stitch in the first stitch. This corresponds to s1 stitch in Row 1 of the 2 sts decrease. Continue as above ending with 6 sts. Cast off.

Back

Using long tail cast on method and size 4mm (6 US) needles cast on 93 (103, 113, 123, 133) sts. Next row: Complete set up row for Gazebo Lace Pattern.

RS row: Start Row 1 of Gazebo Lace pattern or chart. Work to row 18 to complete lace pattern. Continue to repeat Row 17 and Row 18 of pattern until 4" (10. 2 cm) from beginning before starting body shaping.

Body shaping Reduce 1 st at each end of the row 2 (4, 4, 5, 6) times as follows: For size S every 22 rows; Size M every 12 rows; and Sizes L-2X every 10 rows. Work in pattern without decrease until work measures 11 ½ (12, 12 ½, 13, 14)" (29.2 [30.5, 31.8, 33, 35.6]) cm from beginning. Next row: Increase 1 st at each end of the row 91 (97, 105, 115, 123) sts. Work in pattern without increases until work measures 13 ½ (14, 14 ½, 15, 16)" (34.3 [35.6, 36.8, 38.1, 40.6]) cm from beginning. Cast off edge loosely until 3 sts remain on the needle to create the back band.

Horizontal back band Create a band with the 3 sts as follows: Slip the first stitch purlwise, purl, then knit the last stitch. Turn and repeat this instruction until the band is the horizontal length of the back cast off edge. Cast off and sew to the back edge.

Shoulder bands Using long tail cast on and 4mm (6 US) needles cast on 8 sts. Slip the first stitch purlwise, purl 6 and knit the last stitch. Continue in this pattern until the band measures the required length. Make 2. Note: This band is sewn to the back of the cami and to the horizontal back band so when measuring include enough length to sew in.

Finishing

Weave in ends. Sew side seams together. Sew straps to front edge. Attach straps to the inside edge of the back panel and sew again to affix to the back band.

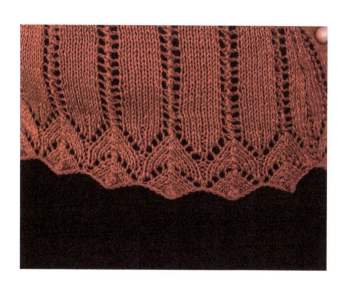

Schematic

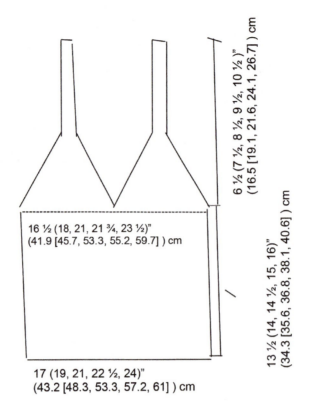

Gazebo Lace Chart

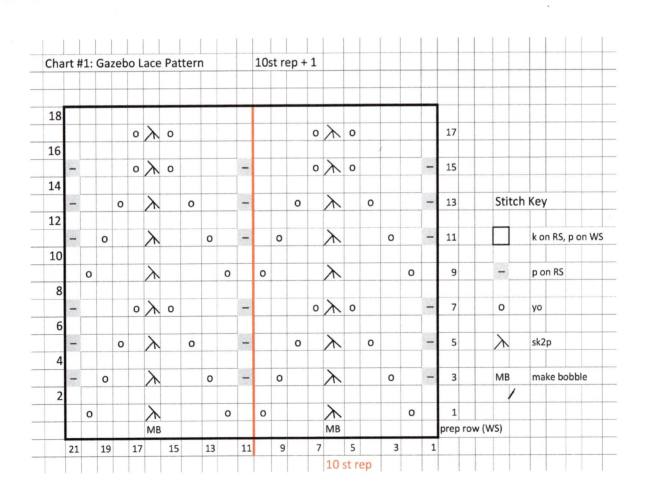

Silk Linen Singlet

The yummy summer colours of this silk linen blend say, "place me close to the skin but gently lay at the hips" – a shell for those warm sunny days; wear with a green skirt or neutral cropped pants and sandals. I wanted this design to flow rather than sit tight against the body. It is shaped wide at the bottom and then gently tapered to the bustline.

Challenge Level	INTERMEDIATE
Finished Bust Size	S (M, L, XL, 2X) 36 (40, 44, 48, 51 ½)" (91.4 [101.6, 111.8, 121.9, 130.8]) cm
Yarn	3 (3, 4, 4, 4) – 65 / 35 Silk Linen blend 115g /4oz. 448m/490yds in alpine meadow by Sarah Elizabeth Fibreworks, Rossland, BC, CANADA.
Needles & Notions	3 ¼mm (3 US) 14" (35.6 cm) straight needles and 24" (60 cm) circular; stitch holder; tapestry needle.
Gauge	25 sts and 33 rows in 4 " (10cm) in stockinette pattern using 3 ¼mm (3 US) needles.
Care Instructions	Hand wash with a gentle wash product. Lie flat, block and air dry.

Bottom Border Pattern

Row 1 (RS): S1, *k2, p2; repeat from *, end with k1.
Row 2: S1, purl to last stitch, k1.
Row 3: S1, *k1, p1; repeat from *, end with k1.
Row 4: Purl.
Row 5: S1, k1, *p2, k2 repeat from * to end.
Row 6: Purl.
Rows 7 (RS): Purl.

Midriff Border Pattern

Row 1 (RS): S1, purl to last stitch, k1.
Row 2: S1, *k2, p2, repeat from *, end with k1.
Row 3: S1, knit.
Row 4: S1, *k1, p1; repeat from *, end with k1.
Row 5: S1, knit to end.
Row 6: S1, *k2, p2; repeat from * end with k1.
Rows 7 (RS): Purl.

INSTRUCTIONS

Front

Using long tail cast on method with Size 3 ¼mm (3 US) needles cast on 116 (134, 146, 158, 170) sts.

Note: Cast on includes 2 selvage stitches; slip the first stitch of every row and knit the last stitch of every row.

Purl next row.

Complete the Bottom Border Pattern. Change to stockinette stitch and begin waist shaping as follows:

Decrease 1 st each end of the 22 (18, 16, 16, 15) row. Repeat this decrease 4 (5, 6, 6, 7) times. 108 (124, 134, 146, 156) sts. When work measures 12" (30.5 cm) from the cast on edge complete the Midriff Border Pattern.

Work again in stockinette stitch until work measures 14 ½ (14 ½, 15 ½, 15 ½, 16 ½)" (36.8 [36.8, 39.4, 39.4, 41.9]) cm before armhole shaping.

Armhole shaping At the start of the next several rows decrease 5 sts, then 4 sts, then 3 sts, then 2 sts, then 1 st 7 (8, 10, 12, 14) times. In addition, for sizes M-2X: Reduce 1 st every 4th row 1 (2, 3, 4) times. 66 (78, 82, 88, 92) sts. At the same time, when 3 ½ (4, 4 ½, 5 ¼, 5 ½) " (8.9 [10.2, 11.4, 13.3, 14]) cm has been completed from armhole cast off, shape the neck edge as follows:

Neck shaping Knit 24 (31, 34, 38, 41) sts and place these stitches onto a holder. Cast off the centre 18 (16, 14, 12, 10) sts, knit to end. Next row: Purl.

For Size S, M: At neck edge reduce 3 sts, then 2 sts, then 1 st (3 times). 18 (23) sts remain.

For Size L: Reduce neck edge 4 sts, then 3 sts twice. 24 sts

For 1X & 2X sizes: Reduce neck edge 4 sts, then 3 sts twice, then 1 st. 27 (30) sts remain.

Continue with no reductions until work measures 7 ½ (8, 8 ½, 9 ½, 10)" (19.1 [20.3, 21.6, 24.1, 25.4]) cm before completing shoulder shaping.

Shoulder shaping Over the next few rows at the shoulder edge, cast off 6 (8, 8, 9, 10) sts twice, then 6 (7, 8, 9, 10) sts.

Place stitches from the holder back onto the needles. Complete the same reductions at neck edge for this side and then complete shoulder shaping.

Back

Using long tail cast on method and size 3 ¼ mm (3 US) needles, cast on 116 (134, 146, 158, 170) sts. Note: Pattern includes 2 selvage stitches – slip the first stitch of every row and knit the last stitch of every row.

Next Row: Purl.

Complete the Bottom Border Pattern. Change to stockinette stitch placing a marker at 38 (45, 49, 53, 57) sts and 76 (90, 98, 106, 114) sts to prepare for dart shaping. Work straight without decreases, slipping markers.

Decrease row: At row 22 (18, 16, 16, 15) work to 2 sts before marker, k2tog, slip marker, work to next marker, slip marker, ssk, knit to end of row. 2 sts decreased. Repeat another 22 (18, 16, 16, 15) rows and complete the decrease row as above. Complete this decrease row: 2 (3, 4, 4, 5) times more. 108 (124, 134, 146, 156) sts. Work without decreases to 14 ½ (14 ½, 15 ½, 15 ½, 16 ½)" (36.8 [36.8, 39.4, 39.4, 41.9]) cm before armhole shaping.

Armhole shaping At the start of the next several rows decrease 5 sts, then 4 sts, then 3 sts, then 2 sts, then 1 st 7 (8, 10, 12, 14) times. In addition, for sizes M-2X: Reduce 1 st every 4th row 1 (2, 3, 4) times. 66 (78, 82, 88, 92) sts. Work until armhole measures 5 ½ (6, 6 ½, 7 ½, 8)" (14 [15.2, 16.5, 19.1, 20.3]) cm from the start of armhole shaping before completing neck shaping.

Neck shaping Knit 24 (31, 34, 38, 41) sts and place onto a holder. Cast off the centre 18 (16, 14, 12, 10) sts, knit to end. Next row: Purl.

For Size S, M: At neck edge reduce 3 sts, then 2 sts, then 1 st 3 times. 18 (23) sts remain.

For Size L: Reduce neck edge 4 sts, then 3 sts twice. For 1X & 2X sizes: Reduce neck edge 4 sts, then 3 sts twice, then 1 st. 24 (27, 30) sts. remain.

Continue with no reductions until work measures 7 ½ (8, 8 ½, 9 ½, 10)" (19.1 [20.3, 21.6, 24.1, 25.4]) cm before completing shoulder shaping.

Shoulder shaping Over the next few rows at shoulder edge, cast off 6 (8, 8, 9, 10) sts twice, then 6 (7, 8, 9,10) sts. Place stitches from the holder back onto the needles. Complete the same reductions at back neck edge for this side and then complete shoulder shaping.

NATURE'S KNIT-CH BOOK OF SINGLETS AND LIGHT COVERS

Finishing

Weave in loose ends. Wash in a gentle wash solution and block out. Leave to air dry. Sew fronts to back at shoulders and sides.

Neck finishing With RS facing and circular needle, pick up stitches evenly along the neck edge. Complete the following:
Rnd 1: Purl.
Rnd 2: *Knit 7, k2tog; repeat from * for the round. Knit any additional stitches.
Rnd 3: Purl.
Rnd 4 (Cast off row): Purl 5, p2tog while casting off the row.
Armhole finishing Pick up stitches evenly.
Rnd 1: Purl.
Rnd 2: Knit.
Rnd 3: Purl.
Rnd 4: Cast off loosely.

Repeat for second armhole.

Schematic

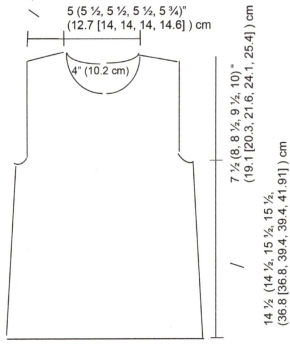

Hemp Sorbet Singlet

The colours remind me of a cool treat on a hot summer day – a bowl of raspberry, peach and coconut sorbets garnished with a few mint leaves. Yum. A summer delight! This shell will get lots of summer sun time, wear with shorts or long flowing skirt and jean jacket.

Challenge Level	■□□□ BEGINNER
Finished Bust Size	S (M, L, XL, 2X, 3X) 35 (37, 39, 43 ½, 48, 52 ½)" (88.9 [94, 99.1, 110.5, 121.9, 133.4]) cm
Yarn	7 (7, 7, 8, 9, 9) - 150m/165y/ 50g allhemp 3 fingering weight, 100% long fibre hemp, Hemp for Knitting designed by Lanaknits, Nelson, BC, CANADA. 1 skein peach; 2(2, 2, 2, 2, 2) skeins white; 2(2, 2, 2, 3, 3) skeins raspberry; 2(2, 2, 2, 3, 3) skeins sprout (spring green).
Needles & Notions	2 ¼mm (1 US) 14" (35.6 cm) straight needles; 24" (60 cm) circular; 1.4mm (8US) crochet hook; stitch holder.
Gauge	32 sts and 48 rows in 4" (10cm) in stockinette pattern using 2 ¼mm (1 US) needles.
Care Instructions	Hand wash with hair shampoo. Lie flat, block and air dry.

1 x 1 Twisted Rib Pattern
(multiple of 2 + selvage)

Row 1: S1, *k1 tbl, p1; repeat from *, k1.

Row 2: S1, k the purl sts and p the knit sts of the previous row knitting into the back of every knit stitch.

INSTRUCTIONS

Front

Using long tail cast on method with Size 2 ¼mm (1 US) needles and peach colour cast on 142 (148, 158, 178, 194, 212) sts. Note: Cast on includes 2 selvage stitches; slip the first stitch of every row and knit the last stitch of every row.

Complete 2" (5.1 cm) of twisted rib stitch pattern ending with a WS row. Change to the white colour and in stockinette stitch complete 4" (10.2 cm) ending with a WS row. Change to the raspberry colour and complete 6" (15.2 cm) ending with a WS row. Change to spring green colour and complete 6 (6, 6 ½, 6 ¾, 7, 7 ¼)" (15.2 [15.2, 16.5, 17.1, 17.8, 18.4]) cm before armhole shaping.

Armhole shaping At the start of the next two rows, cast off 10 (10, 10, 15, 15, 15) sts. For Sizes S-L: Cast off 3 sts, then 2sts, then 1 st 8 (7, 5) times.

For Size XL: Cast off 4 sts, then 3 sts, then 2 sts and 1 st, 3 times. For Size 2X and 3X: Cast off 5st, then 4 sts, 3 sts, 2 sts and 1 st 4 (9) times. 96 (104, 118, 124, 132, 136) sts.

When work measures 3 (3, 3 ½, 4, 4 ½, 5)" (7.6 [7.6, 8.9, 10.2, 11.4, 12.7]) cm from beginning of armhole shaping complete front neck edge shaping.

Front neck edge shaping Complete the following: Work 32 (34, 40, 42, 44, 48) sts and place on a holder, cast off the centre 32 (36, 38, 40, 40, 40) sts and work to end of the row. Next row (WS): Purl. At the neck edge reduce 1 st 12 (14, 16, 18, 18, 20) times. Work without decrease until armhole measures 8 (8, 8 ½, 9, 9 ½, 10) ". Cast off remaining 20 (20, 24, 24, 26, 28) sts.

Complete right front as follows: Place stitches from the holder back on to left needle with the purl-side facing, attach yarn and complete a 1 st reduction at the neck edge 12 (14, 16, 18, 18, 20) times. Work without decrease until armhole measures 8 (8, 8 ½, 9, 9 ½, 10)" (20.3 [20.3, 21.6, 22.9, 24.1, 25.4]) cm. Cast off remaining 20 (20, 24, 24, 26, 28) sts.

Back

Using long tail cast on method with Size 2 ¼mm (1 US) needles and peach colour cast on 142 (148, 158, 178, 194, 212) sts. Note: Cast on includes 2 selvage stitches; slip the first stitch of every row and knit the last stitch of every row.

Complete 2" (5.1 cm) of twisted rib stitch pattern ending with a WS row. Change to white colour and in stockinette stitch complete 4" (10.2 cm) ending with a WS row. Change to raspberry colour and complete 6" (15.2 cm) ending with a WS row. Change to spring green colour and complete 6 (6 ½, 6 ¾, 7, 7 ¼)" (15.2 [15.2, 16.5, 17.1, 17.8, 18.4]) cm before armhole shaping.

Armhole shaping At the start of the next two rows, cast off 10 (10, 10, 15, 15, 15) sts. For Sizes S-L: Cast off 3 sts, then 2sts, then 1 stitch 8 (7, 5) times.

For Size XL: Cast off 4 sts, then 3 sts, then 2 sts and 1 st 3 times.

For Size 2X and 3X: Cast off 5sts, then 4 sts, 3 sts, 2 sts and 1 st 4 (9) times. 96 (104, 118, 124, 132, 136) sts.

When work measures 6 (6, 6 ½, 7, 7 ½, 8)" (15.2 [15.2, 16.5, 17.8, 19.1, 20.3]) cm from beginning of armhole shaping complete back neck edge shaping.

Back neck edge shaping Complete the following: Work 30 (30, 34, 34, 38, 38) sts and place on a holder, cast off the centre 36 (44, 50, 56, 56, 60) sts and work to end of row. Next row (WS): Purl. At the neck edge reduce 3 sts, then 2sts, then 1 st 5 times. Work without decrease until armhole measures 8 (8, 8 ½, 9, 9 ½, 10)" [20.3, 21.6, 22.9, 24.1, 25.4]) cm. Cast off remaining 20 (20, 24, 24, 26, 28) sts.

Complete right back as follows: Place stitches from the holder back on to left needle with the purl-side facing, attach yarn and complete a 3 st reduction at the neck edge. Reduce 2 sts and then 1 st 5 times at the neck edge. Work without decrease until armhole measures 8 (8, 8 ½, 9, 9 ½, 10)" [20.3, 21.6, 22.9, 24.1, 25.4]) cm. Cast off remaining 20 (20, 24, 24, 26, 28) sts.

Finishing

Weave in loose ends. Wash in a hair shampoo and block out. Leave to air dry. Sew fronts to back at shoulders and sides.

Neck and armhole finishing Pick up stitches evenly around the neck edge using a 24" (60 cm) circular needle. Complete 2 rounds of k1, p1. Cast off.

With a crochet hook, complete a single chain stitch around both armholes.

Schematic

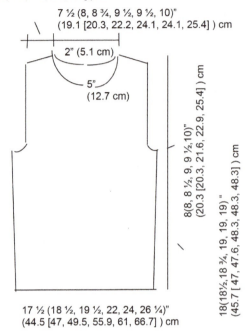

2 ½ (2 ½, 3, 3, 3 ¼, 3 ½)"
(6.4 [6.4, 7.6, 7.6, 8.3, 8.9]) cm

7 ½ (8, 8 ¾, 9 ½, 9 ½, 10)"
(19.1 [20.3, 22.2, 24.1, 24.1, 25.4]) cm

2" (5.1 cm)

5" (12.7 cm)

8 (8, 8 ½, 9, 9 ½, 10)"
(20.3 [20.3, 21.6, 22.9, 25.4]) cm

18 (18½, 18 ¾, 19, 19, 19)"
(45.7 [47, 47.6, 48.3, 48.3, 48.3]) cm

17 ½ (18 ½, 19 ½, 22, 24, 26 ¼)"
(44.5 [47, 49.5, 55.9, 61, 66.7]) cm

NATURE'S KNIT-CH BOOK OF SINGLETS AND LIGHT COVERS — 19

Beaded Loop Shell

A summer fun shell complete with its own beaded necklace! A basic stockinette design for beginner knitters with a slight waist tapering. Knit up in a beautiful blend of cotton, alpaca and wool which is nice and soft against the skin. The beaded loop is knit on after picking up stitches around the neck edge and can be completed without beads.

Challenge Level	■□□□ BEGINNER
Finished Size	S (M, L, XL, 2X, 3X) 37 ½ (40, 43, 47, 51, 55)" (95.3 [101.6, 109.2, 119.4, 129.5, 139.7]) cm
Yarn	4 (4, 5, 5, 6, 6) 100g / 250 yds 3 ply sport 50% cotton, 25% alpaca, 25% Wool, Morrison Creek Farm and Fibre, Courtenay, BC, CANADA.
Needles & Notions	4.0mm (6US) 14" (35.6 cm) straight needles; 24" (60 cm) circular needle; approx. 135-250 Size 2 or 4 glass seed beads; beading needle; stitch holder.
Gauge	21 sts and 32 rows in 4 in. (10 cm) in stockinette pattern using 4.0mm (6 US) needles.
Care Instructions	Hand wash with wool wash or mild detergent. Lie flat, block and air dry.

INSTRUCTIONS

Back

Using long tail cast on method with Size 4.0mm (6 US) needles cast on 102 (110, 118, 128, 139, 149) sts. Establish a k2, p2 pattern and work for 1 ½" (3.8 cm) before changing to stockinette. Note: Pattern includes 2 selvage stitches; on every row slip the first stitch and knit the last stitch.

Work until piece measures 4" (10.2 cm) in length from the cast on row.

Create waist shaping Decrease 1 st each end of the next row as follows: S1, knit 1, k2tog, knit to 4 sts before end of the row, ssk, k2. Work another 2" (5.1 cm) before decreasing 2 sts again on the next row. Work without decrease for another 4" (10.2 cm). Increase 1 st each end on the next row. Continue for another 2" (5.1 cm) before completing another increase row.

Note: You should have the same number of stitches on the needles as at the beginning. Work until piece measures 16" (40.6 cm) from the beginning before completing armhole shaping.

Armhole shaping For Sizes S and M: At the start of the next several rows, cast off 3 sts, then 2 sts, then 1 st 4 (5) times. Work in stockinette until work measures 7 ½ (8)" (19.1 [20.3]) cm from start of armhole shaping before shaping the back neck edge.

For Sizes L to 3X: At the start of the next several rows, cast off 4 sts, then 3 sts, then 2 sts, and 1st 5 (8, 9, 9) times. Work in stockinette until work measures 8 ½ (9, 9 ½, 10)" (21.6 [22.9, 24.1, 25.4])

cm from the start of armhole shaping before shaping the back neck edge.

Neck edge shaping Work 13 (13, 14, 15, 17, 18) sts and place these stitches on a stitch holder. Cast off the centre 55 (62, 62, 64, 64, 69) sts, work to end of row. Purl the next row. At neck edge, reduce 2 sts, knit to end 11 (11, 12, 13, 15, 16) sts. When armhole measures 8 (8 ½, 9, 9 ½, 10, 10 ½)" (20.3 [21.6, 22.9, 24.1, 25.4, 26.7]) cm cast off stitches.

Place right side stitches back on the left needle with purl side facing. Attach yarn reducing 2 sts at neck edge, purl to end of row. Continue in stockinette. When armhole measures 8 (8 ½, 9, 9 ½, 10, 10 ½)" (20.3 [21.6, 22.9, 24.1, 25.4, 26.7]) cm cast off stitches.

Front

Using long tail cast on method with Size 4.0mm (6 US) needles cast on 102 (110, 118, 128, 139, 149) sts. Establish a k2, p2 pattern and work for 1 ½" (3.8 cm) before changing to stockinette.

Note: Pattern includes 2 selvage stitches; on every row slip the first stitch and knit the last stitch.

Work until piece measures 4" (10.2 cm) from cast on edge.

Create waist shaping Decrease 1 st each end of the next row as follows: S1, knit 1, k2tog, knit to 4 sts before end of the row, ssk, k2. Work another 2" (5.1 cm) before decreasing 2 sts again on the next row. Work without decrease for another 4" (10.2 cm). Increase 1 st each end. Continue for another 2" before completing another increase row. Note: You should have the same number of stitches on the needles as at the beginning. Work until piece measures 16" (40.6 cm) from the beginning before completing armhole shaping.

Armhole shaping For Sizes S and M: At the start of the next several rows, cast off 3 sts, then 2 sts, then 1 st 4 (5) times. Work in stockinette until work measures 7 ½ (8)" (19.1 [20.3]) cm from start of armhole shaping before shaping the back neck edge.

For Sizes L to 3X: At the start of the next several rows, cast off 4 sts, then 3 sts, then 2 sts, and 1st 5(8, 9, 9) times. Work in stockinette until work measures 8 ½ (9, 9 ½, 10)" (21.6 [22.9, 24.1, 25.4]) cm from start of armhole shaping before shaping the back neck edge.

Neck edge shaping Work 21 (21, 22, 23, 25, 26) sts and place these stitches on a stitch holder. Cast off the centre 42 (46, 44, 48, 48, 53) sts, work to end of row. Purl the next row. At neck edge, begin reducing 3 sts twice, then 1 st 4 times. 11 (11, 12, 13, 15, 16) sts. When armhole measure 8 (8 ½, 9, 9 ½,10, 10 ½)" (20.3 [21.6, 22.9, 24.1, 25.4, 26.7]) cm cast off stitches.

Place right side stitches back on the left needle with purl side facing. Attach yarn reducing 3 sts twice then 1 st at neck edge 4 times over the next following rows. When armhole measure 8 (8 ½, 9, 9 ½, 10, 10 ½)" (20.3 [21.6, 22.9, 24.1, 25.4, 26.7]) cm cast off stitches.

Finishing

Weave in loose ends. Wash in a wool wash product and block out. Leave to air dry. Sew fronts to backs at shoulders using the shoulder seam stitch.

Beaded loop neck edge Thread the beads on the yarn first using a beading needle.

Starting at the left back neck, right side facing you, pick up stitches along the neck edge with the circular needle ensuring an even number of stitches. Do not join. Next row (WS): Create the beaded loops as follows:

*K1, insert the needle into the next stitch as if to knit (hold the stitch, do not drop the stitch), bring the yarn to the front between the needles, pick up a threaded bead and place between the needles and your left hand thumb. Wrap the yarn around the thumb, then bring the yarn to the back of the work between the needles (creates the loop) while holding the loop on your left thumb. With the right needle, knit into the back of the same stitch dropping the loop now from the thumb. Two stitches have been created and a loop with a bead is between these stitches. Place both of these stitches back onto the left hand needle. Take the second stitch over the first stitch securing the loop. Move the created loop to the back (RS of work).

Continue from * to create the beaded loop fringe. Next row (RS): *k7, k2tog, repeat from * to end to decrease evenly around the neck edge (knit remaining stitches if a full multiple of k7, k2tog cannot be achieved.) As before, create beaded loops again on the front of the shell only, then knit the remaining back stitches.

Cast off row: Purl 1, *p1, place yarn to back of the work, slip the 2 purl stitches back onto the left needle, k2tog tbl. After every 5th purl is completed, P1, p2tog, k2tog tbl. Continue from * until all stitches are cast off. Sew edges of beaded fringe together.

Armhole finishing Sew side seams together. Finish armholes using a single crochet edge.

Schematic

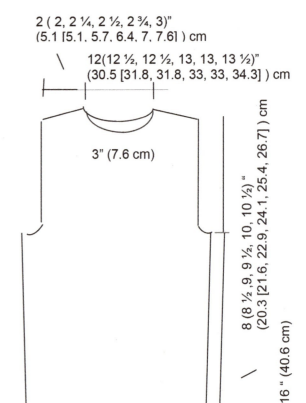

2 (2, 2 ¼, 2 ½, 2 ¾, 3)"
(5.1 [5.1, 5.7, 6.4, 7, 7.6]) cm

12(12 ½, 12 ½, 13, 13, 13 ½)"
(30.5 [31.8, 31.8, 33, 33, 34.3]) cm

3" (7.6 cm)

8 (8 ½, 9, 9 ½, 10, 10 ½)"
(20.3 [21.6, 22.9, 24.1, 25.4, 26.7]) cm

16 " (40.6 cm)

19 (20 ½, 22, 24, 26, 28)"
(48.3 [52.1, 55.9, 61, 66, 71.1]) cm

24 — BEADED LOOP SHELL

Silk Merino Beaded Shell

This shell has come a long way from concept in 2017 to the finish line in November 2021. Two things I knew I wanted – to show off this beautiful silky merino in a soft green hue and bring in a unique method to add some complementary glass beads. The shell has an overskirt addition which adds a slight flare at the bottom of the shell. Wear this elegant shell under a suit jacket and transition it for an evening out with a light wrap.

Challenge Level	**INTERMEDIATE**
Finished Bust Size	S (M, L, XL, 2X) Bust: 33 (36, 42, 43 ¼, 46 ¾)" (83.8 [91.4, 106.7, 109.9, 118.7]) cm Hip: 34 (38, 44, 45, 48)" (86.4 [96.5, 111.8, 114.3, 121.9]) cm
Yarn	3 (3, 3, 4, 4) – 50%silk/50% merino, approx. 435 yds/100g Willy Nilly Silkie Yarn by Wild Geese Fibres, Alberta.
Needles & Notions	3 ¼mm (3 US) circulars in 32" (81.3 cm) and 24" (60 cm); 14" (35.6 cm) straight needles; stitch holder; tapestry needle.
Gauge	30 sts and 32 rows in 4" (10 cm) using repeat of Round 1 of Beaded Rib Twist with 3 ¼mm (3 US) needles.
Care Instructions	Hand wash with a gentle wool wash product. Lie flat, block and air dry.

Stitches Used

2st RT – insert right needle into back of the second stitch on the left needle, make a stitch but do not let it drop, knit into the front of the first stitch on left needle, make a stitch, then move both stitches to right needle.

Wyif – with yarn in front

Tbl – through the back loop

Beaded Rib Twist (multiple of 4 + 3)

Rnd 1: * K4, p3; rep from * to end of rnd.
Rnd 2 &3: Repeat row 1.
Rnd 4: *K4, wyif bring 3 beads up to work, slip the next 3 sts purlwise from left needle, place yarn to the back capturing the 3 beads on RS of work; repeat from * to end of row.
Rnd 5, 6, 7: Repeat Rnds 1, 2 & 3.
Rnd 8: *2 st RT, 2 st RT, p3: rep from * to end.
Repeat Rnds 1-8 for pattern.

INSTRUCTIONS

Front

Thread on 432 (468, 504, 564, 600) No.6 glass beads using a beading needle.

Using long tail cast on method and size 3 ¼mm (3 US) circular needles, cast on 252 (273, 294, 329, 350) sts. Do not join. Next row: purl.

Join the round and establish Beaded Rib Twist pattern. Work pattern for 3 ¾" (9.5 cm) ending with Rnd 8.

Continue now without beading using *k4, p3; repeat from * for pattern. Work until piece measures 12" (30.5 cm) from cast on edge before armhole shaping.

Armhole shaping Divide fronts and backs as equally as possible 126 (137, 148, 165, 175) sts. Place back stitches on to a holder. Complete the following armhole shaping while working in the established pattern for front stitches:

At the beginning of the next following rows for Sizes S-XL: Reduce 5 sts, then 4 sts, then 3 sts, then 2 sts then 1 st 7 (7, 9, 9) times. 84 (95, 102, 102) sts remaining.

For 2X: At the beginning the next following rows reduce 6 sts, then 5 sts, then 4 sts, then 3 sts, then 2 sts and 1 st 9 times. 118 sts remaining.

Work without decrease until piece measures 3 ½ (4, 4 ½, 5, 5 ½)" (8.9

[10.2, 11.4, 12.7, 14]) cm from start of armhole shaping before starting neck edge shaping.

Neck edge shaping K30 (35, 39, 39, 45) sts place on a holder, cast off 24 (25, 24, 24, 28) sts, knit remaining 30 (35, 39, 39, 45) sts. Next row purl. At neck edge reduce 3 sts, 3 times for all sizes.

For Size S: Reduce 2 sts twice, followed by 1 st twice. 15 sts remain.

For Size M, L, XL: Reduce 1 st 9 (8, 8) times. 17 (19, 19) sts remain.

For 2X: Reduce 2 sts twice, then 1 st 7 times. 25 sts remaining.

Continue in established pattern and work until armhole measure 7 ½ (8, 8 ½, 9, 9 ½)" (19.1 [20.3, 21.6, 22.9, 24.1]) cm.

Cast off using the suspended bind off method.

Complete neck edge shaping with the second set of stitches on the holder. Cast off.

Back

Place stitches back on the needles from the holder. Complete the same shaping as specified for the front.

Work to 5 ½ (6, 6 ½, 7, 7 ½)" (14 [15.2, 16.5, 17.8, 19.1]) cm before shaping the neck edge.

Neck edge shaping K30 (35, 39, 39, 45) sts place on a holder, cast off 24 (25, 24, 24, 28) sts, knit remaining 30 (35, 39, 39, 45) sts. Next row purl. At neck edge reduce 3 sts, 3 times for all sizes.

For Size S: Reduce 2 sts twice, followed by 1 st twice. 15 sts remain.

For Size M, L, XL: Reduce 1 st 9 (8, 8) times. 17 (19, 19) sts remain.

For 2X: Reduce 2 sts twice, then 1 st 7 times. 25 sts remaining.

Continue in established pattern and work until armhole measure 7 ½ (8, 8 ½, 9, 9 ½)" (19.1 [20.3, 21.6, 22.9, 24.1]) cm.

Cast off using the suspended bind off method.

Complete neck edge shaping with the second set of stitches on the holder. Cast off.

Finishing

Weave in ends. Sew side seams together. Sew front and back shoulders together using shoulder seam stitch.

Neck edge and armhole finishing – With RS in front of you, pick up stitches evenly from left side, up left shoulder, around back and down right shoulder and across the front. Rnd 1: Purl. Rnd 2: Knit. Next rnd, cast off purlwise using suspended bind off. Complete finishing for armholes in the same manner.

Bottom Overskirt Thread on 432 (468, 504, 564, 600) No.6 glass beads using a beading needle.

Front overskirt: With RS facing you, pick up stitches along bottom edge to align with centre of armholes 126 (137, 148, 165, 175) sts. Next row: M1L, purl, purl to last stitch, M1R. Note: The increase stitches become the selvage stitches which creates a nice edge for the overskirt. Complete pattern aligned with the body remembering to slip the first stitch and knit the last stitch as follows:

Row 1: *k4, p3; repeat from * to end.

Row 2: Purl.

Row 3: *k4, wyif bring 3 beads up to work, slip the next 3 sts purlwise from left needle, place yarn to the back capturing the 3 beads on RS of work k4; repeat from * to end.

Row 4: Repeat Row 2.

Row 5: Repeat Row 1.

Schematic

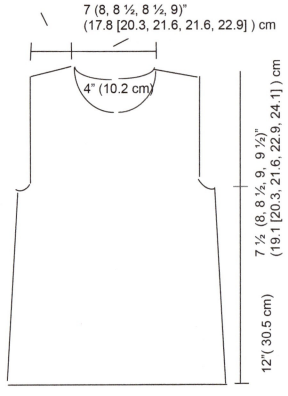

Row 6: Repeat Row 2.

Row 7: *2RT, 2RT, p3; repeat from * to end.

Repeat Row 1-7 until 4 rows of beading are achieved. Then complete Row 1 and 2 once more.

Next 2 rows: Purl.

Next row: knit.

Cast off purlwise as follows: P1, *p1, move yarn to back, slip the 2 sts on right needle onto left needle, k2tog tbl; repeat from * until all stitches are cast off. 3 ½" (8.9 cm).

Back overskirt: Complete the back overskirt following the front overskirt instructions.

Camel / Silk / Alpaca / Merino Singlet

A beautiful bluish purple heather draping softly against the skin. Soft and warm, ready to be worn as a shell underneath a jacket or with a skirt for a summer jaunt. The bottom edges are left open 4" (10 cm) with light detail on the edge. The small detail edge stitch is effective at self-finishing so you don't have to!

Challenge Level	BEGINNER
Finished Bust Size	S (M, L, XL, 2X, 3X) Bust: 34 (38, 44, 47, 52, 54)" (86.4 [96.5, 111.8, 119.4, 132.1, 137.2]) cm
Yarn	4 (4, 5, 5, 6, 6) – 65% suri alpaca/20% camel & silk /15% Merino 2ply, 260yds/100g. Twisted Sisters & Company Fibre Mill, Leduc County, AB.
Needles & Notions	3 ¾mm (5 US) needles; 24" (60 cm) circular needle; stitch holder; tapestry needle.
Gauge	22 sts and 24 rows in 4" (10 cm) in stockinette using 3 ¾mm (5 US) needles.
Care Instructions	Hand wash with a gentle wool wash product. Lie flat, block and air dry.

INSTRUCTIONS

Front

Using long tail cast on method and size 3 ¾ mm (5 US) needles, cast on 90 (104, 118, 124, 138, 145) sts. Next row: Purl.

Establish an edge pattern as follows:

Row 1: S1, k1, *p5, K1; repeat from * ending with p1, k2.

Row 2: S1, p1, k1, *k3, p3; repeat from * ending with k1, p1, k1.

Row 3: S1, k1, p1, k2, *p1, k5; repeat from * ending with p1, k2.

Continue to use s1, k1, p1 for the edge, change to stockinette and finish the row with p1, k2. On every 3rd row add a p1 (s1, k1, p2 knit/purl p2, k2) until work measures 4 ¼" (10.8 cm). Change to stockinette and work 7" (17.8 cm) before bust shaping. Tip: A word about changing skeins. In some cases, with hand dyed yarns, the transition can be glaringly obvious and not desirable. Consider blending the transition by knitting 1 row of new, then 1 row of old for several rows before moving to the new skein.

Bust shaping Increase 1 st each end on the next row 92 (106, 120, 126, 140, 147) sts. Repeat the 2 st increase 3 times every 6th row (8 stitches increased in total). Work without increase until piece measures 16" (40.6 cm) before armhole shaping.

Armhole shaping At the beginning of the next following rows for Sizes S-L: Reduce 4 sts, then 3 sts, then 2 sts, then 1st 3 (6, 10) times. 74 (83, 89) sts remaining. Note: When decreasing 1 st each end establish edge stitches as follows: s1, k1, p1, k2tog, work to last 5 sts before end of row, ssk, p1, k2.

For XL: At the beginning the next following rows reduce 4 sts, then 3 sts twice, then 2 sts and 1st 9 times. 90 sts remaining.

For 2X-3X: At the beginning the next following rows reduce 4 sts twice, then 3 sts twice, then 2 sts

twice and 1st 11 times.
92 (93) sts remaining.

Work without decrease until piece measures 2 (2 ½, 3, 3 ½, 4, 4 ½)" (5.1 [6.4, 7.6, 8.9, 10.2, 11.4]) cm from start of armhole shaping before starting neck edge shaping.

Neck edge shaping s1, k1, p1, k26 (29, 32, 32, 33, 33) sts, cast off centre 22 (25, 25, 26, 26, 27) sts, knit to last 3 sts, p1, k2. Working both sides at the same time, decrease neck edge 3 sts, then 2 sts, then 1 st twice. Work without decreases incorporating s1, k1, p1 along the edge until armhole measures 7 (7 ½, 8, 8 ½, 9, 9 ½)" (17.8 [19.1, 20.3, 21.6, 22.9, 24.1]) cm. Cast off remaining stitches 19 (22, 25, 25, 26, 26) sts.

Back

Using long tail cast on method and size 3 ¾ mm (5 US) needles, cast on 90 (104, 118, 124, 138, 145) sts. Next row: Purl.

Establish an edge pattern as follows:

Row 1: S1, k1, *p5, K1; repeat from * ending with p1, k2.

Row 2: S1, p1, k1,*k3, p3; repeat from * ending with k1, p1, k1.

Row 3: S1, k1, p1, k2, *p1, k5; repeat from * ending with p1, k2.

Continue to use s1, k1, p1 for the edge, change to stockinette and finish the row with p1, k2. On every 3rd row add a p1 (s1, k1, p2 knit/purl p2, k2) until work measures 4 ¼" (10.8 cm). Change to stockinette and work 7" (17.8 cm) before back shaping.

Back shaping Increase 1 st each end on the next row 92 (106, 120, 126, 140, 147) sts. Repeat the 2 st increase 3 times every 6th row (8 stitches increased in total). Work without increase until piece measures 16" (40.6 cm) before armhole shaping.

Armhole shaping At the beginning of the next following rows for Sizes S-L: Reduce 4 sts, then 3 sts, then 2 sts, then 1st 3 (6, 10) times. 74 (83, 89) sts remaining. Note: When decrease 1 st each end establish edge stitches as follows: S1, k1, p1, k2tog, work to last 5 sts before end of row, ssk, p1, k2.

For XL: At the beginning the next following rows reduce 4 sts, then 3 sts twice, then 2 sts and 1st 9 times. 90 sts remaining.

For 2X-3X: At the beginning the next following rows reduce 4 sts twice, then 3 sts twice, then 2 sts twice and 1st 11 times. 92 (93) sts remaining.

Work without decrease until piece measures 4 (4 ½, 5, 5 ½, 6, 6 ½)" (10.2 [11.4, 12.7, 14, 15.2, 16.5]) cm from start of armhole shaping before starting neck edge shaping.

Neck edge shaping s1, k1, p1, k26 (29, 32, 32, 33, 33) sts, cast off centre 22 (25, 25, 26, 26, 27) sts, knit to last 3 sts, p1, k2. Working both sides at the same time, decrease neck edge 3 sts, then 2 sts, then 1 st twice. Work without decreases incorporating s1, k1, p1 along the edge until armhole measures 7 (7 ½, 8, 8 ½, 9, 9 ½)" (17.8 [19.1, 20.3, 21.6, 22.9, 24.1]) cm. Cast off remaining stitches 19 (22, 25, 25, 26, 26) sts.

Finishing

Weave in ends. Sew side seams together. Sew front and back shoulder seams together.

Armhole finishing Crochet a single chain stitch from front armhole decrease to back armhole decrease.

Neck edge Pick up stitches along the neck edge evenly. Next Rnd: Purl. Next Rnd: Cast off knitwise.

Schematic

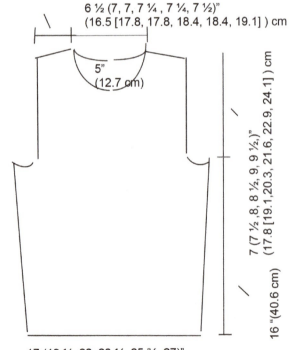

3 ½ (4, 4 ½, 4 ½, 4 ¾, 4 ¾)"
(8.9 [10.2, 11.3, 11.3, 12.1, 12.1]) cm

6 ½ (7, 7, 7 ¼ , 7 ¼, 7 ½)"
(16.5 [17.8, 17.8, 18.4, 18.4, 19.1]) cm

5"
(12.7 cm)

7 (7 ½, 8, 8 ½, 9, 9 ½,)"
(17.8 [19.1, 20.3, 21.6, 22.9, 24.1]) cm

16 "(40.6 cm)

17 (19 ¼, 22, 23 ¼, 25 ¾, 27)"
(43.2 [48.9, 55.9, 59.1, 65.4, 68.6]) cm

Soliloquy Lace Tee

Beauty speaks for itself. This lace pattern is so intriguing and so worth the effort. The wool/cotton blend shows it so well. I sourced this yarn from a small knitting shop in Arizona. The company is Cestari Sheep and Wool Company, USA and they produce from their farm. It is nice to know that they feel the same way about their yarns as we do. Use what is in your backyard.

Challenge Level	■■■□ **INTERMEDIATE**
Finished Bust Size	S (M, L, XL, 2X, 3X) Bust: 38 (42, 46, 50, 54, 58)" (96.5 [106.7, 116.8, 127, 137.2, 147.3]) cm
Yarn	3 (3, 4, 4, 4, 5) – Heather Collection, 75% Cotton/25% Wool in Natural White, 3.5oz., 100g / 250yds. Cestari Sheep and Wool Company, Swoop, VA USA.
Needles & Notions	4.5mm (7 US) 14" (35.6 cm) straight needles; 24" (60 cm) circular; tapestry needle.
Gauge	23 sts and 28 rows in 4" (10cm) using lace pattern.
Care Instructions	Hand wash with a gentle wash product. Lie flat, block and air dry.

INSTRUCTIONS

Front

Using long tail cast on method and size 4.5mm (7 US) straight needles, cast on 114 (123, 132, 150, 159, 168) sts. Note: 2 selvage stitches are included; on every row slip the first stitch and knit the last stitch. Next row: Purl.

Establish a hem pattern by starting at Row 25 of the Lace pattern and working to Row 32. Repeat this set 2 more times. Work should measure 3 ¾" (9.5 cm) from the cast on row.

Begin to work the chart Rows 1-32 until work measures 13 ½ (14, 14 ½, 15, 15 ½, 16)" (34.3 [35.6, 36.8, 38.1, 39.4, 40.6]) cm from cast on edge before adding on for the sleeves.

Sleeves At the end of the last purl row, cable cast on 25 sts. Turn to RS of work, s1, k1, p2, then establish 1 full pattern repeat (18+4) working

the first stitch of the body (normally slipped) as the last stitch of pattern repeat. Then work across the body following the pattern. Turn to WS, using purl cable cast on create 25 sts for the other sleeve. Complete a purl row as you work in the established pattern. Work the body and these addition stitches until work measures 4 ¼ (4 ¾, 5 ¼, 5 ¾, 6 ¼, 6 ½)" (10.8 [12.1, 13.3, 14.6, 15.9, 16.5]) cm before shaping neck edge. 164 (173, 182, 200, 209, 218) sts.

Neck edge shaping Note: We will work both sides at the same time so wind another ball in anticipation. Work 62 (66, 68, 77, 80, 84) sts, cast off centre 41 (42, 45, 46, 49, 50) sts, work to end of row.

Work both sides at the same time as follows:

On every knit row, reduce 1 st at the neck edge 4 times 58 (62, 64, 73, 76, 80) sts. Note: As you decrease watch your balance of yarn overs to k2tog / ssk, when this balance cannot be completed, knit the stitches.

Work straight without shaping until sleeve measures 8 ¾ (9 ¾, 10 ¼, 10 ¾, 11)" (22.2 [24.8, 26, 27.3, 27.9]) cm from sleeve cast on. Cast off stitches using suspended bind off technique.

Back

Using long tail cast on method and size 4.5mm (7 US) straight needles, cast on 114 (123, 132, 150, 159, 168) sts. Note: 2 selvage stitches are included; on every row slip the first stitch and knit the last stitch. Next row: Purl.

Establish a hem pattern by starting at Row 25 of the Waving Cable Lace pattern and working to Row 32. Repeat this set 2 more times. Work should measure 3 ¾" (9.5 cm) from cast on row.

Begin to work the chart Rows 1-32 until work measures 13 ½ (14, 14 ½, 15, 15 ½, 16)" (34.3 [35.6, 36.8, 38.1, 39.4, 40.6]) cm from cast on edge before adding on for the sleeves.

Sleeves At the end of the last purl row, cable cast on 25 sts. Turn to RS of work, s1, k1, p2, then establish 1 full pattern repeat (18+4) working the first stitch of the body (normally slipped) as the last stitch of pattern repeat. Then work across the body following the pattern. Turn to WS, using purl cable cast on create 25 sts. for the other sleeve. Complete a purl row of the established pattern. Work the body and these addition stitches until work measures 6 ¾ (7 ¼, 7 ¾, 8 ¼, 8 ¾, 9)" (17.1 [18.4, 19.7, 21, 22.2, 22.9]) cm before shaping neck edge. 164 (173, 182, 200, 209, 218) sts.

Neck edge shaping Note: we will work both sides at the same time so wind another ball in anticipation. Work 62 (66, 68, 77, 80, 84) sts, cast off the centre 41 (42, 45, 46, 49, 50) sts, work to end of row.

Work both sides at the same time as follows:

On every knit row, reduce 1 st at the neck edge 4 times 58 (62, 64, 73, 76, 80) sts. Note: As you decrease watch your balance of yarn overs to k2tog / ssk, knit the stitches when this balance cannot be completed.

Work straight without shaping until sleeve measures 8 ¾ (9 ¾, 10 ¼, 10 ¾, 11)" (22.2 [24.8, 26, 27.3, 27.9]) cm from sleeve cast on. Cast off stitches using suspended bind off technique.

Finishing

Weave in ends. Sew side seams together. Sew front and back at shoulders.

Neck edge and armhole finishing With RS in front of you, pick up stitches evenly from left side to shoulder seam, around back and down right side and across the front. Complete neck edge finishing as follows:

Rnd 1: Purl.
Rnd 2: *Knit 7 sts, k2tog, repeat from * for the round. Knit any additional stitches.
Rnd 3: Purl.
Rnd 4 (Cast off row): Purl 5 sts, p2tog while casting off the row using suspended bind off technique.

Schematic

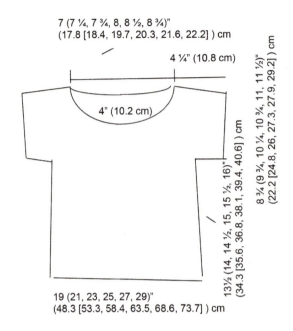

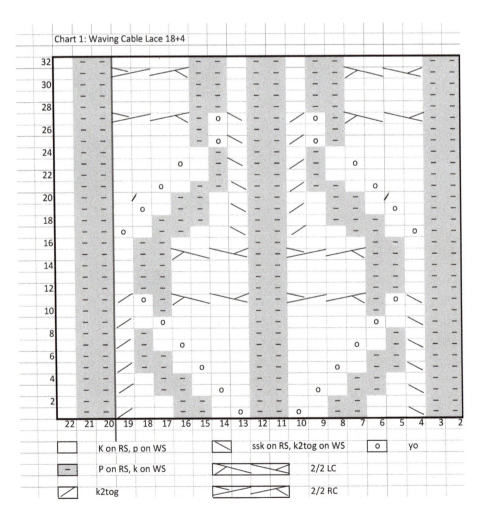

42 — SOLILOQUY LACE TEE

Lovely Locks Shell

What started out as an idea on the back of a paper bag at the Calgary Fibre Arts Show in 2018 is now a treasured design. The use of an art yarn is the focal point of this shell. It presents a challenge in terms of hanging it as a layer on a blend of hemp / cotton with silk, but the results are stunning.

Challenge Level	EXPERIENCED
Finished Bust Size	S (M, L, XL, 2X) Bust: 40 (44, 48, 52, 56)" (101.6 [111.8, 121.9, 132.1, 142.2]) cm
Yarn	2 (3, 3, 3, 4) – Hemp / Cotton (Chanvre /Coton 2/8) 60% organic cotton, 40% Hemp CA-04573, 227g, Homespun Haven, Armstrong, BC, Canada. 1 (1, 1, 1, 1) Mulberry Silk -2ply, 950yds/100g, Homespun Haven, Armstrong, BC Canada. 1 (1, 2, 2, 2) 32 yds, 125g Gotland core spun over a wool/mohair core in grey, white, cream by Sarah Elizabeth Fibre Works, Rossland, BC.
Needles & Notions	3 ¼mm (3 US) 14" (35.6 cm) straight needles; 35mm 12" (30.5 cm) needles; tapestry needle; collar interfacing.
Gauge	24 sts and 34 rows in 4" (10 cm) using 3.25mm needles (3 US) in stockinette holding together 1 strand of silk with 1 strand of Hemp / cotton. 5 sts and 5 rows in 4" (10 cm) using 35mm needles and core spun locks in pattern for locks.
Care Instructions	Hand wash with a gentle wool wash product. Lie flat, block and air dry.

Lace Pattern for Locks
Row 1: * Yo, k2tog; repeat from * to end.
Row 2-4: Knit.

INSTRUCTIONS

Front

Using long tail cast on method and size 3 ¼mm (3 US) straight needles, cast on 122 (134, 146, 158, 170) sts using 1 strand of 2 ply silk and 1 strand of 2 ply hemp / cotton held together. Note: 2 selvage stitches are included; on every row slip the first stitch and knit the last stitch of every row. Next row: Purl.

Establish a k1, p1 ribbing pattern and work for 3" (7.6 cm). Change to stockinette working to 4" (10.2 cm) before completing the waist shaping.

Waist shaping At the beginning of the next rows reduce 1 st each end as follows: S1, k1, ssk; knit to last 4 sts, k2tog, k2. Work in this manner reducing 2 sts at each end every 9th row (1" [2.5 cm]) twice more. 6 sts decreased. Then, work 1" (2.5 cm) and increase 1 st each end. Repeat this 3 times. Work to 13 (13 ½, 14, 14 ½, 15)" (33 [34.3, 35.6, 36.8, 38.1]) cm from cast on before shaping the armhole.

Armhole shaping Over the next few rows at the start of the row, reduce 5 (5, 5, 5, 5) sts, then 4 (4, 4, 4, 4) sts. Then complete shaping for size specified:

For Size M: Reduce 1 st. 122 sts

For Size L-2X: Reduce 3 (3, 3) sts, then 2 (2, 2) sts, then 0 (0, 1) st. 134 (146, 158) sts.

Shape raglan by reducing 1 st each end every other row until work measures 10" (25.4 cm) wide. Armhole length should be 6 (6 ¼, 6 ½, 7, 7 ½) (15.2, [15.9, 16.5, 17.8, 19.1]) cm from start of armhole cast off. Cast off stitches using suspended bind off technique.

Back

Using long tail cast on method and size 3 ¼mm (3 US) straight needles, cast on 122 (134, 146, 158, 170) sts using 1 strand of 2 ply silk and 1 strand of 2 ply hemp / cotton held together. Note: 2 selvage stitches are included; on every row slip the first stitch and knit the last stitch. Next row: Purl.

Establish a k1, p1 ribbing patternand work for 3" (7.6 cm). Change to stockinette working to 4" (10.2 cm) before completing the waist shaping.

Waist shaping At the beginning of the next row reduce 1 st each end as follows: s1, k1, ssk; knit to last 4 sts, k2tog, k2. Work in this manner reducing 2 sts at each end every 9th row (1" [2.5 cm]) twice more. 6 stitches decreased. Then, work 1" (2.5 cm) and increase 1 st each end. Repeat this 3 times. Work to 13 (13 ½, 14, 14 ½, 15)" (33 [34.3, 35.6, 36.8, 38.1]) cm from cast on before shaping the armhole.

Armhole shaping Over the next few rows at the start of the row, reduce 5 (5, 5, 5, 5) sts, then 4 (4, 4, 4, 4) sts. Then complete shaping for size specified:

For Size M: Reduce 1 st. 122st

For Size L-2X: Reduce 3 (3, 3) sts, then 2 (2, 2) sts, then 0 (0, 1) st. 134 (146, 158) sts.

Shape raglan by reducing 1 st each end every other row until work measures 10" (25.4 cm) wide. Armhole length should be 6 (6 ¼, 6 ½, 7, 7 ½)" (15.2, [15.9, 16.5, 17.8, 19.1]) cm from start of armhole cast off. Cast off stitches using the suspended bind off technique.

Collar Band

Using long tail cast on method and size 3 ¼ mm (3 US) straight needles, cast on 104 (116, 122, 131, 134) sts. Work in stockinette until work measure 3 ¼" (8.3 cm) ending with a WS row. Next row: Purl on RS to create a turning row. Complete another 3 ¼" (8.3 cm) before casting off using the suspended bind off technique.
Locks Using a knit cast on, 35mm needles and core spun locks, cast on 42 (47, 49, 53, 54) sts. Purl next row. Next row: Begin pattern for the locks. Complete pattern until work measures 6" (15.2 cm). Cast off loosely.

Finishing

Weave in ends. Sew side seams together.

Sew collars to front and back matching centre front and centre back respectively. Note: Insert a bit of interfacing in the collar to help hold the locks. Sew collar facing to inside.

Sew the locks to the upper edge of the collar by picking up the first row of the lace ensuring to capture the core of the yarn.

Schematic

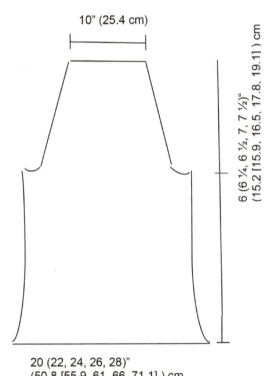

ALPACA LACE SINGLET

This 3ply alpaca is perfect next to the skin – silky, soft, luxurious. Lace details add that feminine touch. This could be worn as evening wear with a long skirt or during the day with a short skirt.

Challenge Level	INTERMEDIATE
Finished Bust Size	S (M, L, XL, 2X, 3X) Bust: 36 (40, 44, 48, 52, 54)" (91.4 [101.6, 111.8, 121.9, 132.1, 137.2]) cm
Yarn	3 (4, 4, 5, 6, 6) – 100% 3ply alpaca, 250yds/100g. Twisted Sisters & Company Fibre Mill, Leduc County, AB.
Needles & Notions	4.0mm (6 US) needles; 3 ½mm 24 " (60 cm) circular needle and dpns; stitch holder; tapestry needle.
Gauge	20 sts and 32 rows in 4" (10cm) in lace pattern using 4.0mm (6 US) needles; 22st and 30 rows in 4" (10cm) using stockinette stitch.
Care Instructions	Hand wash with a gentle wash product or hair shampoo. Lie flat, block and air dry.

INSTRUCTIONS

Front

Using long tail cast on method and size 4.0 mm (6 US) needles, cast on 86 (98, 110, 122, 134, 146) sts. Note: Pattern includes 2 selvage stitches; on every row slip the first stitch and knit the last stitch.

Knit the next 3 rows before starting lace pattern.

Establish lace pattern (Chart 1). Work 2 pattern repeats (28 rows of pattern) before switching to stockinette stitch. Work until front measures 12 (13, 14, 15, 16, 16) in. (30.5 [33, 35.6, 38.1, 40.6, 40.6]) cm from cast on edge before starting armhole shaping.

Armhole shaping At the beginning of the next following rows for Sizes S-L: Reduce 4 sts, then 3 sts, then 2 sts, then 1st 3 (4, 5) times. 62 (72, 82) sts remaining.

For XL: At the beginning the next following rows reduce 5 sts, then 4 sts, then 3 sts, then 2 sts and 1 st 3 times. 88 sts remaining.

For 2X-3X: At the beginning the next following rows reduce 6 sts, then 5 sts, then 3 sts, then 2 sts and 1 st 3(6) times. 96 (104) sts remaining.

Work without decrease until piece measures 4 (4 ½, 5, 5 ½, 6, 6 ½) " (10.2 [11.4, 12.7, 14, 15.2, 16.5]) cm from start of armhole shaping before starting neck edge shaping.

Neck edge shaping S1, k14 (19, 21, 24, 26, 29) sts, cast off centre 34 (34, 40, 40, 44, 46) sts, knit to end of row. Working both sides at the same time, decrease neck edge 3 sts, then 2 sts, then 1 st. Work without decreases until armhole measures 8 (8 ½, 9, 9 ½, 10, 10 ½)" (20.3 [21.6, 22.9, 24.1, 25.4, 26.7]) cm before shoulder shaping. Over the next 3 rows complete the following for each shoulder strap: Cast off 3 (5, 5, 6, 7, 8) twice, then 2 (4, 5, 6, 6, 7) sts.

Back

Using long tail cast on method and size 4.0 mm (6 US) needles, cast on 86 (98, 110, 122, 134, 146) sts. Note: pattern includes 2 selvage stitches; on every row slip the first stitch and knit the last stitch.

Knit the next 3 rows before starting lace pattern.

Establish lace pattern (Chart 1). Work 2 pattern repeats (28 rows of pattern) before switching to stockinette stitch. Work until back measures 12 (13, 14, 15, 16, 16)" (30.5 [33, 35.6, 38.1, 40.6, 40.6]) cm from cast on edge before starting armhole shaping.

Armhole shaping At the beginning of the next following rows for Sizes S-L: Reduce 4 sts, then 3 sts, then 2 sts, then 1st 3 (4, 5) times. 62 (72, 82) sts remaining.

For XL: At the beginning the next following rows reduce 5 sts, then 4 sts, then 3 sts, then 2 sts and 1st 3 times. 88 sts remaining.

For 2X-3X: At the beginning the next following rows reduce 6 sts, then 5st, then 3 sts, then 2 sts and 1st 3 (6) times. 96 (104) sts remaining.

Work without decrease until piece measures 6 (6 ½, 7, 7 ½, 8, 8 ½)" (15.2 [16.5, 17.8, 19.1, 20.3, 21.6]) cm from start of armhole shaping before starting neck edge shaping.

Neck edge shaping s1, k14 (19, 21, 24, 26, 29) sts, cast off centre 34 (34, 40, 40, 44, 46) sts, knit to end of row. Working both sides at the same time, decrease neck edge 3 sts, then 2 sts, then 1 st. Work without decreases until armhole measures 8 (8 ½, 9, 9 ½, 10, 10 ½)" (20.3 [21.6, 22.9, 24.1, 25.4, 26.7]) cm before shoulder shaping. Over the next 3 rows complete shoulder shaping: Cast off 3 (5, 5, 6, 7, 8) twice, then 2 (4, 5, 6, 6, 7) sts.

Finishing

Weave in ends. Sew side seams together. Sew front and back shoulder seams together.

Neck edge i-cord bind off: Pick up stitches around the neck edge as follows:

With right side facing you and 3 ½mm circular needle, start at left shoulder strap picking up stitches along the edge increasing 1 st for every 4 sts picked up. When you have reached the back horizontal edge, pick up stitches without any increase, then begin increasing 1 st every 4 sts again as you make your way up the right back shoulder and down the front shoulder strap. As for the back, pick up the horizontal stitches of the front neck edge without increasing.

Establish i-cord bind off as follows: Once you have reached the first stitch cast on, create 2 extra stitches on the left needle using the cable cast on method. Work as follows:
Step 1: Knit the 2 additional stitches, k2tog.
Step 2: Place the 3 stitches back onto the left needle.
Repeat steps 1 and 2 until 3 sts remain. K2tog, place the stitch back on the left needle and k2tog again. Secure last stitch. Weave in ends.

Armhole finishing Complete armhole finishing as described for the neck edge i-cord bind off.

Finish the second armhole in this manner.

Attaching i-cords to front collar With a darning needle and yarn, thread the needle with yarn through the stitch where you would like to attach the i-cord (visually you have picked up around the "V"). Note: I suggest maintaining a vertical line from the neck edge i-cord as your starting point. With the darning needle tip, pull the yarn up through the "V" creating your first stitch of the i-cord. Place this stitch on a 3 ½mm dpn. Complete the process once more. 2 sts are now on your dpn. Create a third stitch using the cable cast on method. Work the 3 sts now creating the desired length of the i-cord. Place a simple knot at the bottom, knit a few more rounds and cast off. If you are using beads, add these prior to placing the simple knot.

Schematic

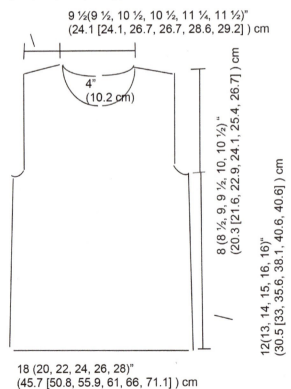

1 ½ (2 ½, 3, 3 ½, 4, 4 ½)"
(3.8 [6.4, 7.6, 8.9, 10.2, 11.4]) cm

9 ½ (9 ½, 10 ½, 10 ½, 11 ¼, 11 ½)"
(24.1 [24.1, 26.7, 26.7, 28.6, 29.2]) cm

4"
(10.2 cm)

8 (8 ½, 9, 9 ½, 10, 10 ½)"
(20.3 [21.6, 22.9, 24.1, 25.4, 26.7]) cm

12 (13, 14, 15, 16, 16)"
(30.5 [33, 35.6, 38.1, 40.6, 40.6]) cm

18 (20, 22, 24, 26, 28)"
(45.7 [50.8, 55.9, 61, 66, 71.1]) cm

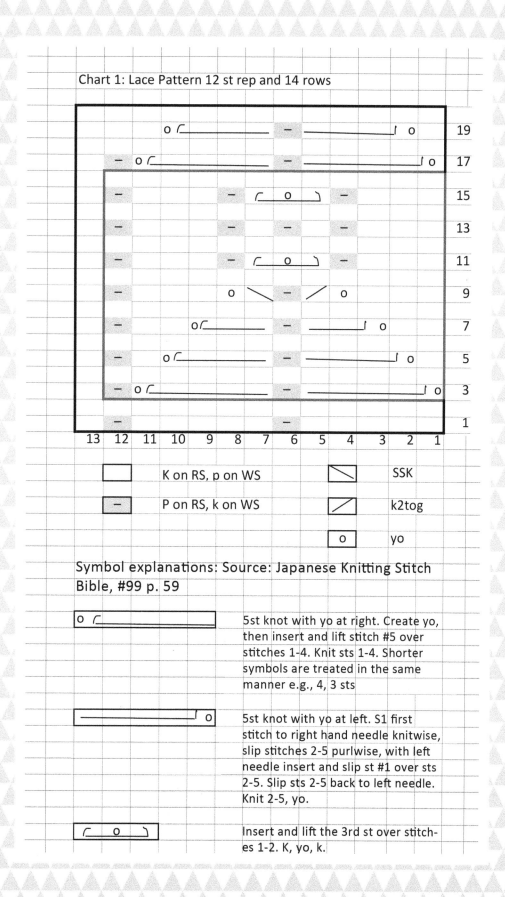

Chart 1: Lace Pattern 12 st rep and 14 rows

Symbol	Meaning
(blank)	K on RS, p on WS
−	P on RS, k on WS
╲	SSK
╱	k2tog
o	yo

Symbol explanations: Source: Japanese Knitting Stitch Bible, #99 p. 59

o ⌐————	5st knot with yo at right. Create yo, then insert and lift stitch #5 over stitches 1-4. Knit sts 1-4. Shorter symbols are treated in the same manner e.g., 4, 3 sts
————¬ o	5st knot with yo at left. S1 first stitch to right hand needle knitwise, slip stitches 2-5 purlwise, with left needle insert and slip st #1 over sts 2-5. Slip sts 2-5 back to left needle. Knit 2-5, yo.
⌐ o ¬	Insert and lift the 3rd st over stitches 1-2. K, yo, k.

Buttoned Peplum Shell

This shell was one of my last designs for the book. I wanted to showcase this mohair fibre coming from a friend that raises mohair goats in Alberta. She is extremely talented at dying skeins. The vibrant colours are a joy to work with. I elected to bead the bodice with pearl glass beads. Button loops are created using a single chain crochet as you knit the button band.

Peplums are figure flattering. This can be worn throughout the year with short or long sleeves underneath or alone with a skirt.

Challenge Level	INTERMEDIATE
Finished Bust Size	S (M, L, XL, 2X, 3X) Bust: 36 (40, 44, 48, 52, 54)" (91.4 [101.6, 111.7, 121.9, 132.1, 137.2]) cm
Yarn	4 (5, 6, 6, 7, 7) – 70% mohair, 30% merino 2 ply 172yds/100g. Mountain Sunset Angoras, Pincher Creek, AB. Two colours- 1 (2, 2, 2, 2, 2) dark and 3 (3, 4, 4, 5, 5) light teal green.
Needles & Notions	4.0mm (6 US) needles; 24" (60 cm) circular needle, 2.35mm (US 1) crochet hook; stitch holder; tapestry needle; approx. 200 #6 glass seed beads; 9-5/8" buttons.
Gauge	19 sts and 26 rows in 4" in stockinette using 4.0mm (6 US) needles.
Care Instructions	Hand wash with a gentle wool wash product. Lie flat, block and air dry.

Wave Pattern

Row 1 (RS): S1, *p1, k5; repeat from * end with k1.

Row 2 (WS): S1, *k1, p1, k1, p3; repeat from * ending with k1.

Row 3: S1, *k2, p1, k1, p1, k1; repeat from * ending with k1.

Row 4: S1, k3, *p1, k5; repeat from * ending with k1.

INSTRUCTIONS

Left Front

Using long tail cast on method and size 4.0 mm (6 US) needles, cast on 38 (44, 50, 56, 62, 68) sts. Note: pattern includes 2 selvage stitches; on every row slip the first stitch and knit the last stitch.

Knit the next row before starting wave pattern.

Establish wave pattern (Chart 1). Work 2" (5.1 cm) in pattern before shaping peplum.

At the start of the next row, s1, k2tog, work to end while remaining in pattern. Complete this decrease twice more after completing 8 rows of the wave pattern (2 repeats). 35 (41, 47, 53, 59, 65) sts. When work measures 6 ½" (16.5 cm) end on a RS row from the cast on edge, transition to light yarn as follows:

Next 2 rows: Knit in the dark colour. Attach new light colour and purl the next two rows before changing to stockinette stitch. If you want to add beads to the bodice - follow the optional beading section at this point.

Work 12 rows in stockinette before starting the bust line increase. On the 13th row, s1, M1, knit to end. Continue increase 1 st at the armhole edge side 4 more times every 8 (9, 9, 9, 10, 11, 12) row 40 (46, 52, 58, 64, 70) sts. Work without increase until work measures 13 ½ (14, 14 ½, 15, 15 ½, 16)" (34.3 [35.6, 36.8, 38.1, 39.4, 40.6]) cm from cast on edge before shaping armhole.

Armhole & neck edge shaping At the beginning of the next following rows for Sizes S-L: Reduce 3 sts, then 2 sts, then 1 st 5 (6, 8) times. 30 (34, 34) sts remaining.

For XL-3X: At the beginning the next following rows reduce 4 sts, then 3 sts, then 2 sts, then 1st 2 (3, 4) times. Then 1 st every 4th row 3 times. 44 (49, 54) sts remaining.

At the same time as armhole shaping, start neck edge shaping as follows:

At neck edge, s1, k1, k2tog, work to end of row. Continue to decrease at neck edge every other row until 18 (19, 21, 22, 24, 25) shoulder sts remain. Work until armhole measures 7 ½ (8, 8 ½, 9, 9 ½, 10)" (19.1 [20.3, 21.6, 22.9, 24.1, 25.4]) cm from start of armhole shaping.

Shoulder shaping Over the next several rows, cast off 6 (6, 7, 7, 8, 8) sts twice, then 6 (7, 7, 8, 8, 9) sts.

Right Front

Using long tail cast on method and size 4.0 mm (6 US) needles, cast on 38 (44, 50, 56, 62, 68) sts. Note: pattern includes 2 selvage stitches; on every row slip the first stitch of and knit the last stitch.

Knit the next row before starting wave pattern.

Establish wave pattern (Chart 1). Work 2" (5.1 cm) in pattern before shaping peplum.

Work to last 3 sts of the row, k2tog, k1. Complete this decrease twice more after completing 8 rows of the wave pattern (2 repeats). 35 (41, 47, 53, 59, 65) sts. When work measures 6 ½" (16.5 cm) ending on a RS row from the cast on edge, transition to light yarn as follows:

Next 2 rows: Knit in the dark colour. Attach new light colour and purl the next two rows before changing to stockinette stitch. If you want to add beads to the bodice, follow Optional Beading at this point.

Work 12 rows in stockinette before starting the bust line increase. On the 13th row, work to last stitch, m1, k1. Continue increasing 1 st at the armhole edge side 4 more times every 8 (9, 9, 9, 10, 11, 12) rows. 40 (46, 52, 58, 64, 70) sts. Work without increase until work measures 13 ½ (14, 14 ½, 15, 15 ½, 16)" (34.3 [35.6, 36.8, 38.1, 39.4, 40.6]) cm from cast on edge before shaping armhole.

Armhole & neck edge shaping At the beginning of the next following rows for Sizes S-L: Reduce 3 sts, then 2 sts, then 1st 5 (6, 8) times. 30 (34, 34) sts remaining.

For XL-3X: At the beginning the next following rows reduce 4 sts, then 3 sts, then 2 sts, then 1 st 2 (3, 4) times. Then 1 st every 4th row 3 times. 44 (49, 54) sts remaining.

At the same time as armhole shaping, start neck edge shaping as follows:

At neck edge, s1, k1, k2tog, work to end of row. Continue to decrease at neck edge every other row until 18 (19, 21, 22, 24, 25) sts remain. Work until armhole measures 7 ½ (8, 8 ½, 9, 9 ½, 10)" (19.1 [20.3, 21.6, 22.9, 24.1, 25.4]) cm from start of armhole shaping.

Shoulder shaping Over the next several rows, cast off 6 (6, 7, 7, 8, 8) sts twice, then 6 (7, 7, 8, 8, 9) sts.

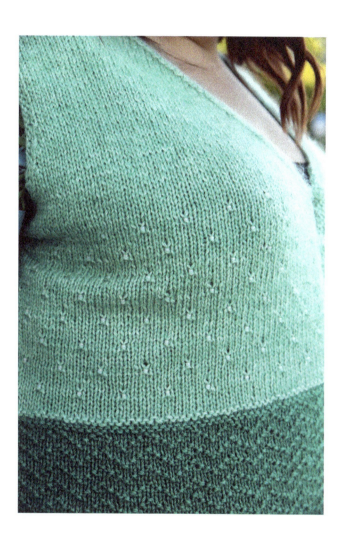

Back

Using long tail cast on method and size 4.0 mm (6 US) needles, cast on 86 (92, 104, 110, 122, 128) sts.

Knit the next row before starting wave pattern.

Establish wave pattern (Chart 1). Work 2" (5.1 cm) in pattern before shaping peplum.

Reduce 1 st each end of the next row. Repeat this decrease twice more when 8 rows of the pattern are completed 80 (86, 98, 104, 116, 122) sts. When work measures 6 ½" (16.5 cm) from cast on edge, complete transition to light yarn.

Work 12 rows in stockinette before starting the back increase. On the 13th row, increase 1 st each end of the row. Continue increasing 1 st at each side 4 more times every 8 (9, 9, 9, 10, 11, 12) row 90 (96, 108, 114, 126, 132) sts. Work without increase until work measures 13 ½ (14, 14 ½, 15, 15 ½, 16)" (34.3 [35.6, 36.8, 38.1, 39.4, 40.6]) cm from cast on edge before shaping armhole.

Armhole shaping At the beginning of the next following rows for Sizes S-L: Reduce 3 sts, then 2 sts, then 1st 5 (6, 8) times. 70 (72, 82) sts remaining.

For XL-3X: At the beginning the next following rows reduce 4 sts, then 3 sts, then 2 sts, then 1st 2 (3, 4) times. Then 1 st every 4th row 3 times. 86 (96, 100) sts remaining.

Work without decrease until armhole measures 7 ½ (8, 8 ½, 9, 9 ½, 10)" (19.1 [20.3, 21.6, 22.9, 24.1, 25.4]) cm from start of armhole shaping.

Shoulder shaping Over the next several rows at each end, cast off 6 (6, 7, 7, 8, 8) sts twice, then 6 (7, 7, 8, 8, 9) sts. Cast off remaining 34 (36, 40, 42, 45, 50) sts of the back neck.

Optional Beading

After the colour transition rows, complete 5 rows of stockinette ending with a RS row. Next row (WS): Follow the low point of the wave in the peplum below – s1, k1, *p5, k1; repeat from * ending with k1. Next row: On each purl stitch slip a bead over the stitch using a fine crochet hook. Note: Note all beads are not the same, if you are struggling to place a bead, try another one as you may find it slips over the stitch with ease. Once the bead is placed, slip the beaded stitch. Continue in this manner, creating a purl-stitch seat for the bead every 5th row, and offsetting the placement of the bead. Work as desired e.g., I completed 8 rows of approximately 10 beads each. At the same time, complete the bustline increase as described for left front. Work to 13 ½ (14, 14 ½, 15, 15 ½, 16)" (34.3 [35.6, 36.8, 38.1, 39.4, 40.6]) cm from cast on edge before starting armhole and neck shaping.

Finishing

Weave in ends. Sew side seams together. Sew front and back shoulder seams together.

Buttonband (Right side) With right side facing you, pick up stitches along centre front in the dark colour increasing 1 st every 4 sts Note: pick up the "V" along the edge, then pick up the back leg of the stitch to create the extra stitch), then switch to the light colour to neck edge. Next row (WS): Knit.

Create button loops On the next row knit and create button loops as follows: At premeasured intervals (½" (1.3 cm) from bottom, and approx. 1 ½" (3.8 cm) between each loop, use a crochet hook to create a 7 st single chain. Insert the hook into the working stitch. Create 7 sts. Bring the chain back to the original knit stitch recreating the knit stitch. Place knit stitch back on right hand needle. Continue in this manner until all button loops have been created. Complete another knit row. Cast off knitwise using suspended bind off method.

Collar Pick up stitches around the neck edge right side facing you, increase 1 st for every 4 sts picked up.

Next row: Purl. Next row: Knit.

As you complete the back, decrease 1 st every 7 sts as follows: Complete 7 sts, then slip the next two stitches onto the right needle, slip the first stitch over the second on the needle, place the stitch back on the left needle and continue to complete another 7 sts. Do this only for the back, then complete front stitches without decreases.

Row 3: Purl.

Row 4 (Cast off row): Purl 5, p2tog while casting off the row.

Armhole finishing Pick up stitches around the armholes right side facing you with circular needles. Purl next round, knit, then cast off stitches purlwise.
Finish the second armhole in this manner.

Schematic

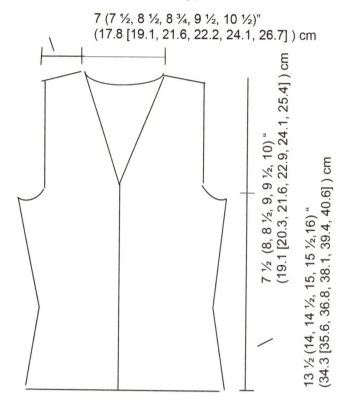

3 ¾ (4, 4 ¼, 4 ½, 5, 5 ¼)"
9.5 [10.2, 10.8, 11.4, 12.7, 13.3]) cm

7 (7 ½, 8 ½, 8 ¾, 9 ½, 10 ½)"
(17.8 [19.1, 21.6, 22.2, 24.1, 26.7]) cm

7 ½ (8, 8 ½, 9, 9 ½, 10)"
(19.1 [20.3, 21.6, 22.9, 24.1, 25.4]) cm

13 ½ (14, 14 ½, 15, 15 ½, 16)"
(34.3 [35.6, 36.8, 38.1, 39.4, 40.6]) cm

18 (19 ¼, 22 ,23 ¼, 25 ¾, 27)"
(45.7 [48.9, 55.9, 59.1, 65.4, 68.6]) cm

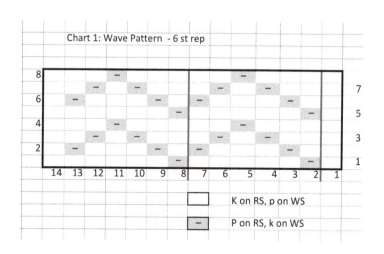

Light Cover Ups

Runners Sleeveless Kanga.................. p. 65
Hemp Lace Beachcomber .... p. 71
Beaded Hemp Ruana .... p. 77
Summer Breeze Vest – Version 3 .... p. 83
Neo .... p. 91
In the Garden Pullover..................... p. 97
Solstice Kimono.............................. p. 103
Leaf .... p. 111
Cozy Cabled Cardi .... p. 117
Round We Go Cardi .... p. 125

Runner's Sleeveless Kanga

For those nippy days when a bit of extra breathable warmth is required. This hip length kanga is ribbed under the arms and sides to ensure it does not impede any arm movement. A little extra width is provided for the bust line and buttocks to ensure good coverage.

Challenge Level	▰▰▰▱ INTERMEDIATE
Finished Bust Size	S (M, L, XL, 2X) Bust: 32 (36, 40, 44, 48)" (81.3 [91.4, 101.6, 111.8, 121.9]) cm
Yarn	4 (4, 5, 5, 6) – 112g/226m (247 yds) 2ply natural local wool, brown/grey(llama), Heart West Haven, Priddis, AB, CANADA.
Needles & Notions	4 ½mm (7 US) 14" (35.6 cm) straight needles, 24" (60 cm) circular needle; tapestry needle.
Gauge	20 sts and 28 rows in 4" (10 cm) using 4 ½mm needles and stockinette stitch.
Care Instructions	Hand wash with a gentle wool wash product. Lie flat, block and air dry.

Stitches Used

f&b – knit/purl into the front and back of the stitch to increase by 1 st.

w&t – at desired point on the RS row, place yarn in front, slip the next stitch purlwise, place yarn to the back, turn the work to begin WS row.

INSTRUCTIONS

Front

Using long tail cast on method and size 4 ½mm (7 US) straight needles, cast on 82 (92, 102, 112, 122) sts. Note: 2 selvage stitches are included; on every row slip the first stitch and knit the last stitch. Next row: Purl.

Complete 2 (2 ½, 2 ½, 3, 3)" (5.1 [6.4, 6.4, 7.6, 7.6]) cm of k1, p1 ribbing.

Begin the body section as follows: Continue to rib the first 10 (10, 13, 14, 15) sts, then change to stockinette until the last 10 (10, 13, 14, 15) sts remain. Complete these in rib pattern. Continue in this manner until work measures 6 (6 ½, 7 ½, 8, 8 ½)" (15.2 [16.5, 19.1, 20.3, 21.6]) cm from the start of the body section.

Increase for bust: Complete rib 10 (10, 13, 14, 15) sts, in the next stitch K1 f&b to create an extra stitch, continue to 1 st before rib section, K1 f&b, complete rib to end (2 sts added). Continue rib, stockinette, rib pattern treating the addition stitches as an extension of the rib section. Repeat this increase row every 6th row 4 more times (10 sts increased in total). 92 (102, 112, 122, 132) sts. When work measures 13 (14, 15, 16, 16 ½)" (33 [35.6, 38.1, 40.6, 41.9]) cm from cast on edge complete armhole shaping.

Armhole shaping For Size S: Cast off 4 sts at armhole edge, then 3 sts, 2 sts and 1 st 2 times. 70 sts remain.

For Size M: Cast off 3 sts at armhole edge, then 2 sts, then 1 st 3 times. 86 sts remain.

For Size L-2X: Cast off 4 sts at armhole edge, then 3 sts twice, then 2 sts, then 1 st 2 (6, 8) times. 28 (36, 40) sts decreased. 84 (86, 92) sts remain.

At the same time, when work measures 1 ½ (2 ½, 3 ½, 4 ½, 4 ½)" (3.8 [6.4, 8.9, 11.4, 11.4]) cm from armhole shaping cast off 2 sts at the centre front to create centre front slit as follows: Work 34 (42, 41, 42, 45) sts, cast off 2 sts, work to end of row. Work both sides at the same time by joining another ball of yarn on the next row. Work until centre front measures 6" (15.2 cm) from cast off edge before shaping neck edge.

Neck edge shaping At each neck edge cast off 11 (18, 14, 14, 15) sts, work to end. Reduce 3 sts, then 2 sts at the next edge over the next few rows. Work without reduction until armhole measures 7 ½ (8 ½, 9 ½, 9 ½, 10 ½)" (19.1 [21.6, 24.1, 24.1, 26.7]) cm. Cast off remaining 18 (19, 22, 23, 25) sts.

Back

With 4.5 mm (7 US) needles cast on 92 (102, 112, 122, 132) sts. Complete k1, p1 ribbing for 2 (2 ½, 2 ½, 3, 3)" (5.1 [6.4, 6.4, 7.6, 7.6]) cm.

Next row: Complete 19 sts in rib pattern, change to stockinette and work across the row until the last 19sts remain. Complete remaining in rib pattern. Work In this manner until back measures 5 ½" (14 cm) from cast on edge.

At the start and end of every 6th row, decrease 1 st where the ribbing and stockinette meet 5 times. 82 (92, 102, 112, 122) sts.

Continue without shaping until piece measures 13 (14, 15, 16, 16 ½)" (33 [35.6, 38.1, 40.6, 41.9]) cm before completing armhole shaping.

Armhole shaping For Size S: Cast off 3 sts at armhole edge, then 2 sts and 1 st. 70 sts remain.

For Size M: Cast off 2sts at armhole edge, then 1 st. 86 sts remain.

For Size L: Cast off 3 sts, followed by 2 sts, then 1 st 4 times. 84 sts remain.

For XL, 2X: Cast off 4 sts at armhole edge, then 3 sts twice, then 2 sts, then 1 st 1 (3) times. 86 (92) sts remain.

Neck edge shaping Work to 23 (24, 27, 28, 30) sts, cast off 24 (38, 30, 30, 32) sts work to end. Work both sides at the same time, reducing 3 sts, then 2 sts at the neck edge. 18 (19, 22, 23, 25) sts rem. When work measures 7 ½ (8 ½, 9 ½, 9 ½, 10 ½)" (19.1 [21.6, 24.1, 24.1, 26.7]) cm cast off remaining shoulder stitches.

Kanga Pouch

Cast on 54 sts. Complete 3" (7.6 cm) stockinette before shaping. At each RS edge: s1, k1, k2tog, knit to last 4 sts, ssk, k2. Next row: Purl. Continue shaping with these 2 rows until work measures 7" (17.8 cm) from start of work. Complete decreases until 32 sts remain. Work without decreasing for 3 rows. Cast off loosely.

Shaped Hood (short row shaping)

Sew shoulder seams together. Pick up stitches evenly around the next edge 70 (76, 80, 80, 86) sts. Work 1(1, 1, 2, 2)" (2.5 [2.5, 2.5, 5.1, 5.1]) cm in stockinette. Then divide stitches into 3 equal sections as possible e.g., 23 sts / 24 sts /23 sts placing markers.

Complete the first set of short rows as follows starting on a RS row:

Row 1: Work to end of the row to last stitch, wrap and turn; w&t.

Row 2: Purl to the last stitch of the row; w&t.

Row 3: Knit to 1 stitch before last wrapped stitch; w&t.

Row 4: Purl to 1 stitch before the last wrapped stitch; w&t.

Continue to repeat Row 3 and 4 until all stitches outside of the markers have been wrapped.

Next row: Work 2 rows picking up all the wrapped stitches.

Complete the second set of short rows as follows:

Row 1: Work to marker, slip marker, w&t next stitch.

Row 2: Purl to marker, slip marker, w&t next stitch.

Row 3: Work to w&t, pick up wrap and knit the stitch, w&t the next stitch.

Row 4: Purl to the w&t, pick up wrap and purl the stitch, w&t the next stitch.

Continue working Row 3 and Row 4 until 2/3 of the stitches have been picked up after the markers. Note: You can adjust the depth of the hood here by picking up more stitches as desired.

Over the next two rows, pick up all the wrapped stitches and pick up stitches along the hood from the 1-2" (2.5-5.1 cm) knit before the hood shaping. Purl the next row completing the same shaping on the other side. Next row: Cast off using suspended bind off technique.

Finishing

Centre front Finish edge of centre front by picking up stitches evenly along the edge, across the 2 st decrease and up the opposite side. Cast off knitwise. Note: Insert a zipper or leave open.

Kangaroo Pocket Place the kangaroo pocket matching centre fronts and aligning the bottom edge 1" (2.5 cm) from front edge ribbing. Sew in place with thread or 3 ply embroidery floss matching the yarn colour.

Hood i-cord casing Pick up stitches around the hood opening. Work 3 rows in stockinette. On the next RS row, purl the row to create the turning edge, complete 3 more rows, cast off. Sew to underside of hood.

Braided cord Create a braided cord with a contrasting yarn to the length desired. Measure 6 - 2 ½ yd (2.3m) pieces of contrasting yarn. Tie a knot 1" (2.5cm) from one edge, braid holding two strands together until the desired length. Note: Gather up the 2 strands into balls to help facilitate the braiding. Before final tie-off to secure the braid, thread through the hoodie casing to adjust length as required. Tie off the other end. Trim to 1" (2.5 cm).

Sew up side seams. Single crochet around armhole edges to finish.

Schematic

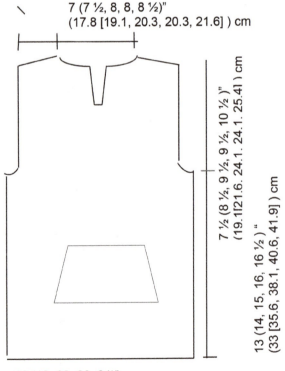

3 ¾(4, 4 ½, 4 ¾, 5)"
(9.5 [10.2, 11.4, 12.1, 12.7]) cm

7 (7 ½, 8, 8, 8 ½)"
(17.8 [19.1, 20.3, 20.3, 21.6]) cm

7 ½ (8 ½, 9 ½, 9 ½, 10 ½)"
(19.1 [21.6, 24.1, 24.1, 25.41]) cm

13 (14, 15, 16, 16 ½)"
(33 [35.6, 38.1, 40.6, 41.9]) cm

16 (18, 20, 22, 24)"
(40.6 [45.7, 50.8, 55.9, 61]) cm

Hemp Lace Beachcomber

Ideal as a beach cover or a light cover for a summer dress. This design is figure flattering, covering your sides and thighs yet shorter at the back so you won't sit on it. Beads (optional) add that extra sparkle and are completed after blocking out the lace.

Challenge Level	INTERMEDIATE
Finished Bust Size	S (M, L, XL) 42 ½ x 18 (52 ½ x 22, 58 x 25 ½, 66 x 27 ½)" (108 x 45.7 [133.4 x 55.9, 147.3 x 64.8, 167.6 x 69.9]) cm
Yarn	3 (4, 5, 5) 50g, 150m / 165yds allhemp3 100%, long staple hemp fibre fingering weight, Hemp for Knitting, Nelson, BC, CANADA.
Needles & Notions	4 ½mm (7US) 29" (73.7 cm) circular; approx. 386 (473, 522, 594) Size 6 glass seed beads; beading needle.
Gauge	22 sts and 19 rows in 4" (10cm) in a blocked Waves Lace pattern using 4 ½mm (7 US) needles.
Care Instructions	Hand wash with a hair shampoo. Rinse thoroughly. Lie flat, block and air dry.

INSTRUCTIONS

Body

Using long tail cast on method with Size 4 ½mm (7 US) circular needles cast on 235 (295, 319, 367) sts. Purl next row, do not join.

Establish pattern as follows: S1, k1, p1, start row 1 of Waves Lace (Chart 1), ending the row with p1, k2. Purl row: S1, p1, k1, complete row 2 of waves lace pattern ending with k1, p1, k1.

Note: The first and last 3 sts of the row create a finish-free frame for this sleeveless cover.

Continue in pattern until work measures 8 (8 ½, 9, 10)" (20.3 [21.6, 22.9, 25.4]) cm before creating armhole openings.

Note: Wind two more balls of hemp as three sections will be worked at the same time to complete armhole openings.

Armhole openings Note: This is where you need to be careful with your lace pattern. Ensure you can balance your yarn overs with cast offs. Use a single decrease when you are repeating only half the lace motif otherwise knit. As you work the three sections, slip the first stitch and knit the last stitch at the armhole edges to create a finish free armhole.

Work the 3 sections simultaneously using the 3 balls. TIP: If you are careful how you turn your work (clockwise versus counterclockwise), you can keep the 3 balls from twisting on each other.

Create bottom of armhole Work the next row of the pattern to 74 (85, 91, 96) sts. Attach a new yarn on next stitch and cast off 6 (11, 17, 22) sts. Work across in pattern until 80 (96, 108, 118) sts remain. Join another yarn and cast-off the other armhole 6 (11, 17, 22) sts. Work to end of row.

Work as established until armhole measures 7 ½ (8 ½, 9, 10)" (19.1 [21.6, 22.9, 25.4]) cm.

Create top of armhole Add back the stitches removed 6 (11, 17, 22) sts to close the armhole opening staying in pattern 235 (295, 319, 367) sts.

Work pattern without decrease completing 1 (2, 2, 3) - 12 row pattern repeat(s) ending with a WS row.

Cast off Purl 1, *p1, place yarn to back of the work, slip the 2 purl stitches back onto the left needle, k2tog tbl. Continue from * until all stitches are cast off.

Finishing

Weave in loose ends. Wash hemp in a hair shampoo, rinse thoroughly and block out the lace to air dry.

Optional beading

Beads are required to bead 2 purl rows at the bottom and 1 purl row at the top of the cover.

Measure a length of hemp. Secure the end of the hemp at the start of where you want the beads to be. Use a beading needle that allows the hemp to easily go through the eye of the needle and is thin enough to allow a bead to slip over needle with the threaded hemp.

Follow the pattern as described and shown below so that a bead occurs every 3 purl sts:

Weave the hemp yarn **up** through the purl stitch **down** through the next purl stitch, **up** through the next, then thread a bead onto the threaded hemp. Place the bead. Be careful not to pull too tightly.

Next, weave the yarn **down** through the next purl stitch, **up** through the next purl stitch and then **down** through the next, place a bead. Continue in this up and down weave until the width of the cover is completed. Complete one more row on the bottom edge and one row on the top edge of the cover.

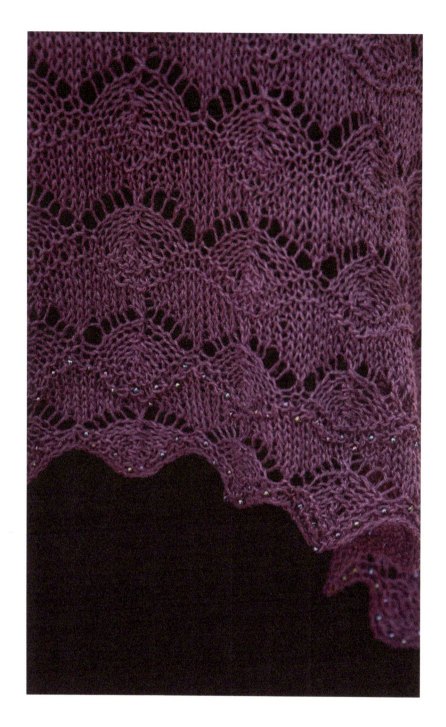

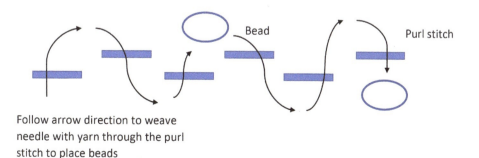

Follow arrow direction to weave needle with yarn through the purl stitch to place beads

Schematic

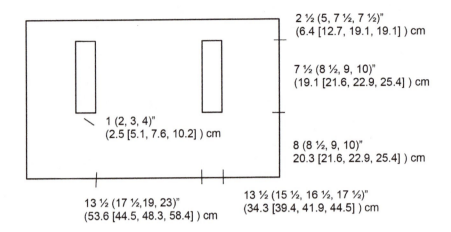

Wave Lace Chart

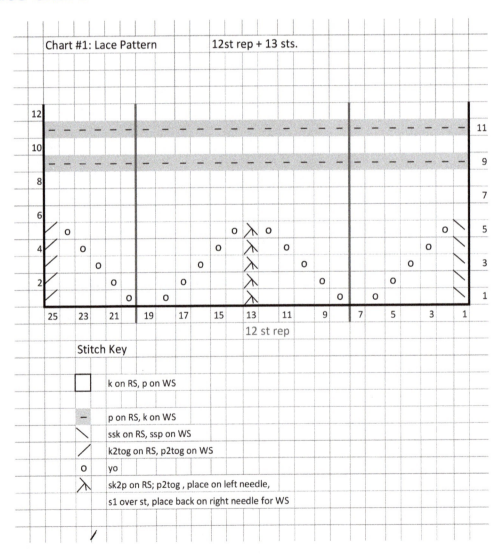

Beaded Hemp Ruana

Akin to our popular Maui poncho. A refreshed look using the same long staple hemp fibre. The two pieces are fully beaded for a lovely drape effect. This piece speaks "beach" but could be a great cover for a summer night stroll. It can be worn with a quarter twist so that shoulder seams lay at centre front and back for more side coverage.

Challenge Level	BEGINNER
Finished Bust Size	One size fits all
Yarn	4 - 150m/165y/ 50g allhemp3 fingering weight, 100% long fibre hemp, Hemp for Knitting, Nelson, BC, CANADA.
Needles & Notions	10.0mm (15US) 14" (35.6 cm) straight needles; approx. 210 size 6 glass seed beads; 70 bugle / barrel wood beads and 400 round wood beads, John Bead Corporation, Toronto, Ontario; beading needle, stitch holder.
Gauge	15 sts and 10 rows in 4" (10cm) in rib stitch pattern using 10.0mm (15 US) needles.
Care Instructions	Hand wash with hair shampoo. Lie flat, block and air dry.

Rib Stitch Pattern (multiple of 6 + 2)

Row 1: K2, *pb1, k1, p1, pbl, k2; repeat from * to end.

Row 2: P2, *kb1, k1, p1, kb1, p2; repeat from * to end.

INSTRUCTIONS

Back

Using knit cast on method with Size 10.0mm (15 US) needles cast on 74 sts. Establish rib stitch pattern and work until piece measures 48" (121.9 cm). Cast off using the suspended bind off method.

Front

Using knit cast on method with Size 10.0mm (15 US) needles cast on 74 sts. Establish rib stitch pattern and work until piece measures 48" (121.9 cm). Cast off using the suspended bind off method.

Finishing

Weave in loose ends. Wash in a hair shampoo and block out. Leave to air dry. Mark centre front and centre back with safety pins. Sew fronts to backs as follows: Match centre front to back, measure 5" (12.7 cm) from centre. Start stitching back and front together at this point using a mattress stitch and work for 8" (20.3 cm). Cast off firmly and weave hemp into the ply. Repeat on the other side.

Note: 6" (15.2 cm) is left open at the shoulder and is beaded.

Schematic

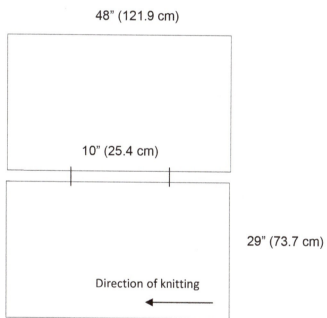

Beaded fringe Starting below the shoulder seam, use a length of yarn with a beading needle and fasten hemp securely. Weave through the edge of the knitting incorporating beads in a regularized pattern as shown:

NATURE'S KNIT-CH BOOK OF SINGLETS AND LIGHT COVERS — 79

Beading Diagram

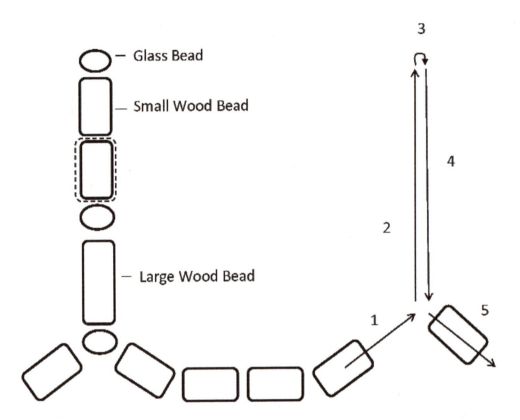

Method is as follows:

1. Thread through the first bead, then a glass bead, the larger bugle / barrel bead, two round wood beads and the final glass bead.

2. Loop the thread over the glass bead to secure and then thread it back through the two round wood beads until the first glass bead is reached.

Make sure all the beads are secured together being careful not to pull the weaving.

3. Continue to weave through the edge of the knitting placing 3 round wood beads as you weave before repeating Step 1.

Repeat the pattern until the whole outside edge of the front and back are complete.

Summer Breeze Vest – Version 3
A Colour Distraction

It is funny how you finish up a design and then wonder what it would look like if I did this...meet the 3rd version of the Summer Breeze Vest – no hood, standing collar and shaping rather than a cinched waist. The impetus to make another version had everything to do with the lovely seafoam green yarn colour!

Challenge Level	INTERMEDIATE
Finished Bust Size	S (M, L, XL, 2X) Bust: 38 (42, 46, 50, 54)" (96.5 [106.7, 116.8, 127, 137.2]) cm
Yarn	4 (4, 5, 5, 6) – 112g /226m (247 yds) 2ply mule spinner yarns, Custom Woolen Mills, Carstairs, AB, CANADA in seafoam green.
Needles & Notions	4 ½mm (7 US) 14" (35.6 cm) straight needles; 24" (60 cm) circular needle; 7 – 1" (2.5 cm) buttons.
Gauge	18 sts and 22 rows in 4" (10 cm) using 4 ½mm needles and stockinette stitch.
Care Instructions	Hand wash with a gentle wool wash product. Lie flat, block and air dry.

Pattern 1

Row 1(RS): Purl.
Row 2: Knit.
Rows 5: *K1, p1, repeat from * to end.
Rows 6: *P1, k1; repeat from * to end.
Row 7: Knit.
Rows 8: Knit.

Pattern 2: Embossed Diamond
(see Chart #1)

Pattern 3

Row 1: Purl.
Row 2: Knit.
Rows 3 & 4: Seed stitch.
Row 5: Knit.
Row 6: Purl.

INSTRUCTIONS

Left Front

Using long tail cast on method and size 4 ½mm (7 US) straight needles, cast on 45 (49, 54, 59, 63) sts. Note: 2 selvage stitches are included; on every row slip the first stitch and knit the last stitch. Next 3 rows: Purl.

Complete Pattern 1.

Continue in stockinette until work measures 8" (20.3 cm) from cast on edge before starting Pattern 2 Embossed Diamond. See Chart #1.

At the same time, create the left side pocket opening as follows:

Work next row until 2 ½" (6.4 cm) from the centre front edge. Cast off 25 sts, complete the row. Next row (WS): Purl to 1 st before the cast-off stitches, then use a purl cable cast on to recover the 25sts previously cast off. Complete the row. Continue to work Pattern 2 Embossed Diamond. Change to stockinette and work 4 rows before creating body shaping.

Body shaping On the next row, work to the middle of your row, pm, ssk, work to end. Continue to shape every 6th row (5 rows in between each shaping) 3 more times. 41 (45, 50, 55, 59) sts. Work without shaping until work measures 7 ½" (19.1 cm) from the end of Pattern 2 before completing armhole shaping.

Armhole shaping For Size S (M): Cast off 3 sts, then 2 sts, then 1 st 3 (5) times at armhole edge. 8 (10) sts decreased.

For Size L (XL): Cast off 4 sts, then 3 sts twice, then 2 sts, then 1 st 1 (0) times at armhole edge. 13 (12) sts decreased.

For Size 2X: Cast off 4 sts, then 3 sts 3 times, then 2 sts, then 1st at armhole edge. 16 sts decreased.

When work measures 5" (12.7 cm) from armhole shaping complete Pattern 3.

Continue in stockinette until work measures 5 ½ (6, 6 ½, 7, 7 ½)" (14 [15.2, 16.5, 17.8, 19.1]) cm from beginning of armhole shaping, then begin neck edge and shoulder shaping.

Neck and shoulder shaping For Size S: At neck edge cast off 4 sts, 3 sts twice, 2 sts twice and 1 st. 15 sts decrease. At the same time, when armhole measures 9" (22.9 cm) cast off 6 sts at the armhole edge 3 times.

For Size M (L): At neck edge cast off 4 sts, 3 sts twice, 2 sts 3 times and 1 st. 17 sts decreased. At the same time, when armhole measures 9 ½ (10)" (24.1 [25.4]) cm cast off 6 (7) sts at armhole edge 3 times.

For Size XL (2X): At neck edge cast off 4 sts, 3 st twice (3 times), 2 sts 4 times and 1 st. 19 (22) sts decreased. At the same time, when armhole measures 10 ½ (11)" (26.7 [27.9]) cm cast off 8 sts at armhole edge twice, then 8 (9) sts.

Pocket Lining On WS with top of opening facing you, pick up 2 sts before the cast-off edge, another 25 sts, then 2 sts for a total of 29 sts. This should leave a purl ridge on the RS that completes the bottom of Pattern 2. Work in stockinette stitch for 5" (12.7 cm). Cast off.

Right Front

Complete as directed for left front reversing all shaping.

Back

With 4 ½mm (7 US) needles cast on 88 (96, 106, 116, 124) sts. Purl next row. Complete Pattern 1. Change to stockinette and work for 5" (12.7 cm) ending with a RS row before creating back shaping. On a WS row, divide the stitches into 4 equal sections to indicate where the shaping will occur. Place a marker between the first and second sections and another marker between the 3rd and 4th sections.

Shaping Row (RS): Knit to 1 st before marker, k2tog, slip marker, work across the last marker, slip marker, ssk, knit to end.

Work another 5 rows before repeating the shaping row once more. 84 (92, 102, 112, 120) sts.

Continue in stockinette until work measures 8" (20.3 cm) from cast on edge. Complete Pattern 2. Work stockinette stitch for 4 rows. On the 5th row, as described previously repeat the shaping row. Again, repeat the shaping row once more after working 5 more rows. 80 (88, 98, 108, 116) sts. Work without shaping for 3" (7.6 cm), then increase 1 st at markers as follows:

Work to last stitch before 1st marker, make 1 (m1), k1, slip marker, work to next marker, slip marker, k1, m1, knit to end. Repeat this row once more after completing 5 rows of stockinette. 84(92, 102, 112, 120) sts.

Work without shaping until piece measures 7 ½" (19.1 cm) measured from the top of Pattern #2 before starting armhole shaping.

Armhole shaping For Size S (M): Cast off 3 sts, then 2 sts, then 1 st 3 (5) times at armhole edge. 8 (10) sts decreased.

For Size L (XL): Cast off 4 sts, then 3 sts twice, then 2 sts, then 1 st 1(0) times at armhole edge. 13 (12) sts decreased.

For Size 2X: Cast off 4 sts, then 3 sts 3 times, then 2 sts, then 1 st at armhole edge. 16 sts decrease.

When work measures 5" (12.7 cm) from armhole shaping complete Pattern 3.

Continue in stockinette until work measures 9 (9 ½, 10, 10 ½, 11)" (22.9 [24.1, 25.4, 26.8, 27.9]) cm from beginning of armhole shaping; then begin shoulder shaping.

Shoulder shaping For Size S: Cast off 6 sts at armhole edge 3 times.

For Size M (L): When armhole measures 9 ½ (10)" (24.1 [25.4]) cm, cast off 6 (7) sts at armhole edge 3 times.

For Size XL (2X): At neck edge cast off 4 sts, 3 sts twice (3 times), 2 sts 4 times and 1 st. 19 (22) sts decreased. At the same time, when armhole measures 10 ½ (11)" (26.7 [27.9]) cm cast off 8 sts at armhole edge twice, then 8 (9) sts.

Finishing

Sew backs to fronts at shoulders and sides.

Collar With right side facing and circular needle, pick up stitches evenly from left front, back and right front. Purl next row. Complete Pattern 1 with the following additions; decrease 1 st (k2tog) after every 5 sts on Row 4, complete the seed stitch section, then on Row 7, decrease 1 st every 4 sts only on the front bands. Complete Row 8. Cast off using suspended bind off method.

Buttonbands With RS facing, pick up stitches evenly along centre front edge.

Row 1 (WS): S1, *purl 3, purl into front and back (f&b) of next stitch; repeat from * ending with k1.

Row 2: Purl on RS.

Row 3: Purl.

Row 4, 5, 6: K1, p1 (seed stitch pattern)

Row 7, 8, 9: Purl.

Row 10: Cast off purlwise.

Complete buttonhole band incorporating 7 buttonholes evenly spaced using the one row buttonhole technique as you complete the first seed stitch row of the above pattern.

Armhole finishing With RS facing, pick up stitches evenly along front armhole edge and down back armhole edge. Purl next row. Cast off knitwise.

Pocket finishing With RS facing, pick up 26 sts along the bottom cast off edge of the pocket opening. Establish rib pattern s1 wyif, *k1, p1; repeat from * ending with k1. Complete 2 rows in rib pattern. Cast off in pattern. Tack pocket trim edges to front. Sew pocket linings to fronts.

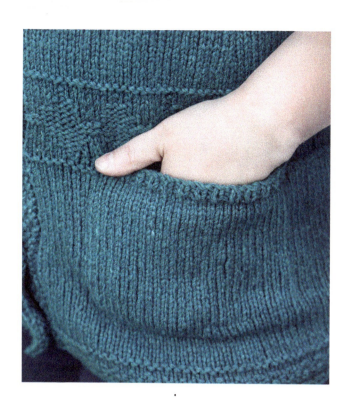

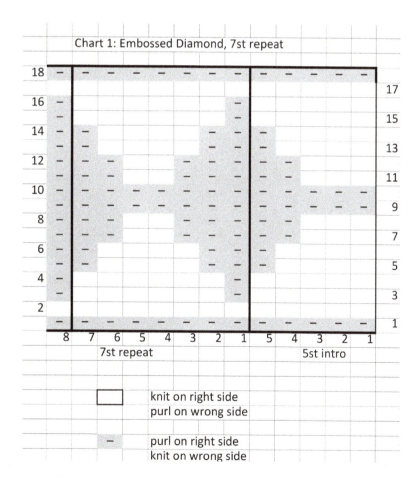

Chart 1: Embossed Diamond, 7st repeat

NATURE'S KNIT-CH BOOK OF SINGLETS AND LIGHT COVERS — 87

Schematic

4 (4, 4 ½, 5 ¼, 5 ½)"
(10.2 [10.2, 11.4, 13.3, 14]) cm

6 ¾ (7 ½, 8 ½, 8 ½, 9 ¾)"
(17.1 [19.1, 21.6, 21.6, 24.8]) cm

2 ½ " (6.4 cm)

9 (9 ½, 10, 10 ½, 11)"
(22.9 [24.1, 25.4, 26.7, 27.9]) cm

19" (48.3 cm)

19 (21, 23, 25, 27)"
(47.5 [53.3, 58.4, 63.5, 68.9]) cm

NEO

I was hooked with just one touch of this 3-ply alpaca. The colours remind me of our Sunday deserts as a child, Neapolitan ice cream…I always wanted more of the vanilla and chocolate as strawberry wasn't a favorite. The design is meant to give lots of air – perfect on a breezy summer day with a singlet underneath.

Challenge Level	INTERMEDIATE
Finished Bust Size	S (M, L, XL, 2X, 3X) Bust: 38 (42, 46, 50, 54, 58)" (96.5 [106.7, 116.8, 127, 137.2, 147.3]) cm
Yarn	4 (4, 5, 5, 6, 7) – 100% alpaca, 310 yds/100g, Twisted Sister & Company Fibre Mill, Leduc County, AB, CANADA.
Needles & Notions	4.0mm (6 US) 14" (35.6 cm) straight needles; 24" (60 cm) circular; stitch holder.
Gauge	21 sts and 24 rows in 4" (10 cm) using 4.0mm needles and Perforated Stitch pattern.
Care Instructions	Hand wash with a gentle hair shampoo. Lie flat to air dry.

Perforated Stitch

(multiple of 4+2+selv, Source: Mon Tricot Knitting Encyclopedia, p.109)

Row 1 (RS): K2, *sl, k1, psso, m1 dbl (wind thread twice around needle), k2tog, rep from *.

Row 2 and all alternate rows: Purl, knitting into the front and back of the "made" stitches.

Row 3: *Sl, k1, psso, m1 dbl, k2tog; repeat from *, k2.

Row 5: Repeat row 1.

INSTRUCTIONS

Front and Back

Using long tail cast on method and size 4.0mm (6 US) straight needles, cast on 100 (108, 124, 128, 140, 152) sts. Note: 2 selvage stitches are included; on every row slip the first stitch and knit the last stitch. Next 3 rows: Knit.

Establish Perforated Stitch pattern.

Work in established lace pattern until work measures 16 (18, 19 ½, 21, 22, 23)" (40.6 [45.7, 49.5, 53.3, 55.9, 58.4]) cm before completing neck edge shaping.

Neck edge shaping Work 40 (43, 50, 51, 58, 61) sts in pattern, place stitches on a holder. Cast off the centre 20 (22, 24, 26, 24, 30) sts work to end. Note: Stay in pattern as much as possible balancing the increases (yo) with the decreases (k2tog, ssk). When this is not possible knit or purl the stitches accordingly.

Left neck edge shaping Over the next several rows at neck edge, complete the following reductions:

For Size S (M): Cast off 4 (4) sts, then 3 (3) sts, then 1 st 7 (7) times. 14 (14) sts reduced.

For Size L: Cast off 5 sts, then 3 sts, then 1 st 12 times at armhole edge. 20 sts decreased.

For Size XL, 2X, 3X: Cast off 6 sts, then 3sts, then 1st 12 times. 21 sts decreased.

Work without further decrease until work measures 16 (18, 19 ½, 21, 22, 23)" (40.6 [45.7, 49.5, 53.3, 55.9, 58.4]) cm from cast on edge. Cast off using suspended bind off method.

Right neck edge shaping Place stitches from holder back onto the needles and complete the neck edge reductions as above.

Work without further decrease until work measures 16 (18, 19 ½, 21, 22, 23)" (40.6 [45.7, 49.5, 53.3, 55.9, 58.4]) cm from cast on edge. Cast off using suspended bind off method.

Size S: Increase 1 st each end every 11th row 8 times.

Size M: Increase 1 st each end every 7th row 12 times.

Size L: Increase 1 st each end every 5th row 16 times.

Size XL (2X): Increase 1 st each end every 4th row 20 (22) times.

Size 3X: Increase 1 st each end every 3rd row 28 times.

Stitch count: 74 (84, 95, 106, 110, 126) sts. Cast off using the suspended bind off method.

Sleeves

With 4.0 mm (6 US) needles cast on 56 (60, 64, 68, 68, 72) sts. Complete 3 rows of knit. Establish Perforated Stitch pattern and complete increases of 1 st each end of the row for the given size while continuing in pattern:

Finishing

Weave in ends, wash and block. Sew backs to fronts at shoulders and sides.

Neck edge finish Pick up stitches with circular needle and RS facing you. Purl next round. Next rnd: *k7, k2tog; repeat from * to end of rnd. Note: knit any extra stitches if there is less than a full multiple.

Next rnd: Purl.

Cast off purlwise completing *p5, p2tog; repeat from * as you cast off.

Schematic

5 (5 ½, 5 ¾, 6 ½, 7, 7 ½)"
(12.7 [14, 14.6, 16.5, 17.8, 19.1]) cm

9 (10, 10 ½, 11 ½, 12 ½, 13 ¾)"
(22.9 [25.4, 26.7, 29.2, 31.8, 34.9]) cm

4"
(10.2) cm

7 (8, 9, 10, 10 ½, 11)"
(17.8 [20.3, 22.9, 25.4, 26.7, 27.9]) cm

13 (14, 14 ½, 15, 15 ½, 16)"
(33 [35.6, 36.8, 38.1, 39.4, 40.6]) cm

19 (21, 23 ½, 25, 27, 29)"
(48.3 [53.3, 59.7, 63.5, 68.6, 73.7]) cm

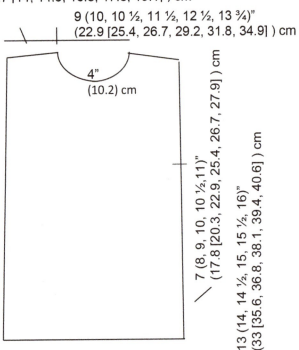

7 (8, 9, 10, 10 ½ , 11)"
(17.8 [20.3, 22.9, 25.4, 26.7, 27.9]) cm

11 (11 ½, 12, 12 ½, 13, 13 ½)"
(27.9 [29.2, 30.5, 31.8, 33, 34.3]) cm

14 (14 ¼, 14 ½, 14 ¾, 15, 15 ¼)"
(35.6 [36.2, 36.8, 37.5, 38.1, 41.3]) cm

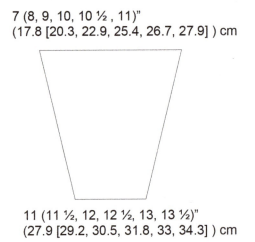

In the Garden Pullover

First of the collection – this pullover has a jacquard patterning completed by duplicate stitch to create the flowers. Just for fun, the colours were randomized by picking them out of a hat! The leaves are knit as the body is worked in the round to the armholes.

Challenge Level	INTERMEDIATE
Finished Bust Size	S (M, L, XL, 2X, 3X) Bust: 34 (36, 38, 42, 46, 50)" (86.4 [91.4, 96.5, 106.7, 116.8, 127]) cm
Yarn	4 (5, 5, 6, 6, 7) – 100% natural wool, 2ply, 112g/226m (247 yds), Mule Spinner Yarns, Custom Woolen Mills Ltd. Carstairs, AB. CANADA in purple haze beige. 1 skein of green, red, pink, purple, and white.
Needles & Notions	5.0mm (8 US) 14" (35.6 cm) straight needles; 29" (73.6 cm) and 24" (60 cm) circulars.
Gauge	16 sts and 22 rows in 4" (10 cm) using 5.0mm (8US) needles in stockinette stitch.
Care Instructions	Hand wash with a wool wash product. Block, lie flat to air dry.

INSTRUCTIONS

Front and Back

Using long tail cast on method and size 5.0mm (8 US) 29" (73.6 cm) circular needles, cast on 153 (162, 171, 189, 207, 225) sts.

Join and work k1, p1 ribbing for 2 ½" (6.4 cm). Change to knit and complete 1" (2.5 cm) ending with a WS row. Next row: Create eyelet border as follows:

Rnd 1: *K2tog, yo; *repeat from * to end of rnd.

Rnd 2: Knit.

Complete 2 rnds of knit before starting pattern motif (Chart #1). Note: you are incorporating the green motif only. Complete 50 rnds of pattern, work 2 rnds of knit, then create eyelet pattern once more. Work in knit until work measures 13 (13 ½, 14, 14 ½, 15, 15 ½)" (33 [34.3, 35.6,

36.8, 38.1, 39.4]) cm from cast on edge before separating back and front at armhole.

Front armhole shaping At the start of the next rnd start front armhole shaping as follows:

Size S-XL: Cast off 4 sts, work 73 (77, 82, 91) sts. Place remaining stitches onto a holder. Work now back and forth using straight needles if desired.

Next row: Cast off 4 sts, purl to end of row.

Over the next several rows complete the following armhole reductions:

Cast off 3 sts, then 2 sts, then 1 st 1 (2, 2, 6) times. 57 (60, 65, 65) sts remaining.

Work without shaping until work measures 2 ½ (3, 3 ½, 4)" (6.4 [7.6, 8.9, 10.2]) cm from start of armhole cast off before beginning neck edge shaping.

Size 2X-3X: Cast off 4 sts, work 100 (109) sts. Place remaining stitches onto a holder. Work now back and forth using straight needles if desired.

Next row: Cast off 4 sts, purl to end of row.

Over the next several rows complete the following armhole reductions:

Cast off 3 sts twice, then 2 sts, then 1 st 5 (6) times. 70 (78) sts remaining.

Work without shaping until work measures 4 ½ (5)" (11.4 [12.7]) cm from start of armhole cast off before beginning neck edge shaping.

Neck edge shaping Work 18 (19, 20, 21, 23, 27) sts, cast off centre 21 (22, 23, 23, 24, 24) sts, knit to end. Working both sides at the same time, purl next left side stitches, attach a new ball and complete right side stitches.

Over the next several rows at neck edge, reduce 3 sts, then 2 sts, then 1 st 5 times. Work without shaping until armhole measures 7 ½ (8, 8 ½, 9, 9 ½, 10)" (19.1 [20.3, 21.6, 22.9, 24.1, 25.4]) cm from the start of armhole shaping. Cast off the remaining 8 (9, 10, 11, 13, 17) sts using suspended bind off method.

Back

Place the stitches from the holder back on 5.0mm (8US) straight needles and complete the following armhole shaping:

Size S-XL: Cast off 4 sts, then 3 sts, then 2 sts, then 1 st 1 (2, 2, 6) times. 57 (60, 65, 65) sts remaining.

Size 2X (3X): Cast off 4 sts, then 3 sts twice, then 2 sts, then 1 st 5 (6) times. 70 (78) sts remaining.

When work measures 7 (7 ½, 8, 8 ½, 9, 9 ½)" (17.8 [19.1, 20.3, 21.6, 22.9, 24.1]) cm shape neck edge.

Neck edge shaping Work 13 (14, 15, 16, 18, 22) sts, cast off centre 31 (32, 33, 33, 34, 34) sts, knit to end. Working both sides at the same time, at the neck edge reduce 3 sts, then 2 sts. Work without further shaping until armhole measures 7 ½ (8, 8 ½, 9, 9 ½, 10)" (19.1 [20.3, 21.6, 22.9, 24.1, 25.4]) cm. Cast off remaining 8 (9, 10, 11, 13, 17) sts.

Sleeves

Using long tail cast on method and size 5.0mm (8 US) straight needles, cast on 40 (40, 43, 43,

45, 45) sts. Work 2 ½" (6.4 cm) in k1, p1 ribbing. Change to stockinette and complete 1" (2.5 cm). Complete 2 rows of eyelet and 2 additional rows in stockinette. After eyelet, incorporate the sleeve pattern (Chart 2) Note: complete green leaf pattern only. Complete 2 rows of stockinette followed by two rows of the eyelet pattern. At the same time: Increase 1 st each end of every 6 (6, 6, 5, 5, 4) rows until 59 (63, 68, 72, 77, 81) sts are on the needles. When sleeve measures 15 ½ (15 ½, 16, 16, 16 ½, 16 ½)" (39.4 [39.4, 40.6, 40.6, 41.9, 41.9]) cm complete armhole shaping.

Armhole shaping For Size S-XL: At the start of the next rows reduce 4 sts, then 3 sts, then 2 sts.

For Size 2X and 3X: reduce 4 sts, then 3 sts twice, then 2 sts.

On every alternating row for all sizes, reduce 1 st each end until work measures 4 ½ (4 ½, 5, 5 ½, 5 ½, 6 ¼)" (11.4 [11.4, 12.7, 14, 14, 15.9]) cm from the start of armhole shaping. 21 (25, 25, 28, 27, 41) sts.

Cap shaping At the start of the next 6 rows decrease 2 sts each end. Cast off remaining 9 (13, 14, 16, 15, 29) sts.

Flower Embellishing

Flowers are created using swiss darning / overstitching. Following stitch placement from chart. Note: Complete darning for inside colours first; working your way out. Have fun with randomizing the colour selection for the flowers. Weave in loose ends.

Finishing

Block and sew shoulder seams.

Neck edge Pick up stitches around the neck edge as follows: Pick up every bound off stitch on each side of the neck edge, pick up 3 sts for every 4 stitches on the straight edge. Complete ½" (1.3 cm) of k1, p1 ribbing. Cast off.

Sew in sleeves and sew sleeve sides together.

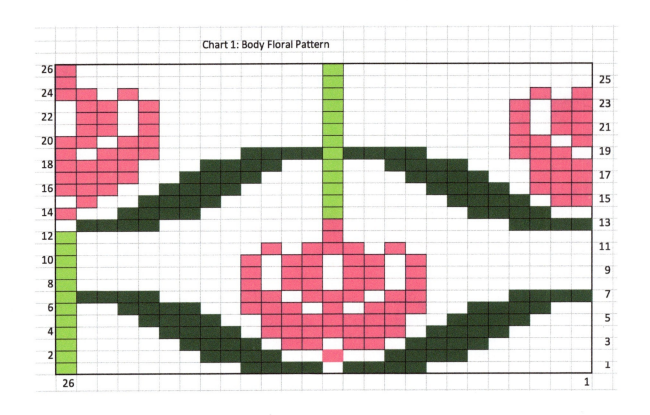

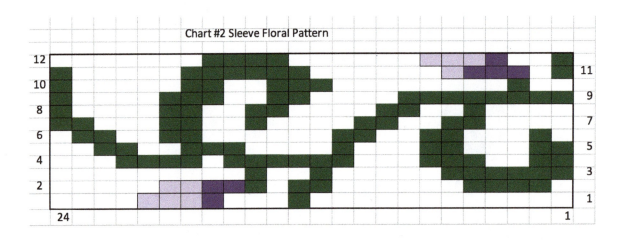

Schematics

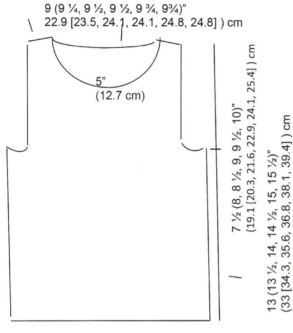

1 ¾ (2, 2 ¼, 2 ½, 2 ¾, 3 ¾)"
4.4 [5.1, 5.7, 6.4, 7, 9.5]) cm

9 (9 ¼, 9 ½, 9 ½, 9 ¾, 9¾)"
22.9 [23.5, 24.1, 24.1, 24.8, 24.8]) cm

5"
(12.7 cm)

7 ½ (8, 8 ½, 9, 9 ½, 10)"
(19.1 [20.3, 21.6, 22.9, 24.1, 25.4]) cm

13 (13 ½, 14, 14 ½, 15, 15 ½)"
(33 [34.3, 35.6, 36.8, 38.1, 39.4]) cm

17 (18, 19, 21, 23, 25)
(43.2 [45.7, 48.3, 53.3, 58.4, 63.5]) cm

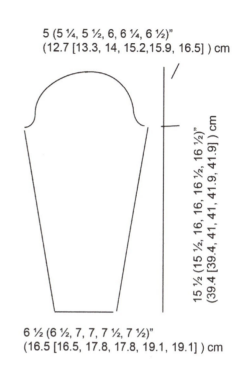

5 (5 ¼, 5 ½, 6, 6 ¼, 6 ½)"
(12.7 [13.3, 14, 15.2, 15.9, 16.5]) cm

15 ½ (15 ½, 16, 16, 16 ½, 16 ½)"
(39.4 [39.4, 41, 41, 41.9, 41.9]) cm

6 ½ (6 ½, 7, 7, 7 ½, 7 ½)"
(16.5 [16.5, 17.8, 17.8, 19.1, 19.1]) cm

Solstice Cable Leaf Kimono

This lovely cover up was designed after a floral kimono that I have had for years. It was my hope that some day I would try to figure out how to convert the floral fabric into a knitted lace pattern. A challenge for another day. The drape of this kimono, cinched at the waist works well with this lovely suri alpaca from Sunnyview Alpacas in Saskatoon. To my delight the cable leaf lace pattern provides a wonderful diagonal patterning to play with. The diagonals move toward the center in the front of the kimono and move outward from a centre cable panel in the back.

Challenge Level	**INTERMEDIATE**
Finished Bust Size	S-XL (2X-3X) 25 ½ x 40 (25 ½ x 42)" (64.8 x 101.6 [64.8 x 106.7]) cm
Yarn	3 (4) – 2ply, 100% suri alpaca, 200g, Sunnyview Alpacas, Clavet, SK, CANADA.
Needles & Notions	3 ½mm (4 US) 14" (35.6 cm) straight needles; seam binding; ¼" (0.64 cm) elastic.
Gauge	24 sts and 32 rows in 4" (10 cm) using 3 ½mm needles and Leaf Cabled lace pattern.
Care Instructions	Hand wash with a gentle hair shampoo or delicate wash. Lie flat to air dry.

INSTRUCTIONS

Left Front

Using long tail cast on method and size 3 ½mm (4 US) straight needles, cast on 103 sts. Note: 2 selvage stitches are included; on every row slip the first stitch and knit the last stitch. Complete 1" (2.5 cm) of garter stitch before starting Leaf Cabled lace pattern.

Next RS row: S1, k5, place a marker, then start row 1 of Leaf Cabled Lace Pattern (Chart 1), repeat pattern 3 times until 2 sts remain, k2. Note: the 2 knit stitches at the end will form part of the centre front 3 sts + selvage garter border. Next Row: s1, k1, complete Row 2 of pattern, complete repeats to marker, knit 6.

Continue building the garter frame and working the lace chart until work measure 25 ½" (64.8 cm) from cast on edge. Cast off in pattern using the suspended bind off method.

Right Front

Using long tail cast on method and size 3 ½mm (4 US) straight needles, cast on 103 sts. Complete 1" (2.5 cm) in garter stitch. Reverse shaping for right front as follows: s1, k1, begin Chart #1 Leaf Cabled Lace pattern at stitch 11-24, then resume repeats, place a marker before the last 6sts, k6. This allows the diagonals of the pattern to flow towards the centre front to mirror the left front patterning.

Continue building the garter frame and working the lace chart until work measure 25 ½" (64.8 cm) from cast on edge. Cast off in pattern using the suspended bind off method.

Back – 2 panels

Left back and centre Using long tail cast on method and size 3 ½mm (4 US) straight needles, cast on 129 (143) sts. Note: the lace pattern on the back moves in the opposite direction of the front.

Work 1" (2.5 cm) in garter stitch. Next RS Row: S1, k5, place marker, work across Row 1 of Chart #1 starting with stitches 11-24, complete 3 repeats, then work across Chart #2 Leaf Cable Centre Panel, repeat the 5st intro, then k1. Continue to work following the charts until left back and centre back measure 25 ½" (64.8 cm) before casing off. Cast off in pattern using the suspended bind off method.

Right Back Using long tail cast on method and size 3 ½mm (4 US) straight needles, cast on 103 sts. Complete 1" of garter stitch before starting lace pattern.

Next RS row: S1, k5, place a marker, then start row 1 of Chart #1: Leaf Cabled Lace Pattern, repeat pattern 3 times until 2 sts remain, k2. Next Row: s1, k1, complete Row 2 of pattern, complete repeats to marker, knit 6.

Continue building pattern until work measure 25 ½" (64.8 cm) from cast on edge. Cast off in pattern using the suspended bind off method.

Finishing

Sew fronts to backs at shoulder seams, leaving approximate 2 ¾" (7 cm) open at the shoulder edge. Sew backs together along selvage edges to create one piece.

Waist cinch Create a casing with seam binding tape as follows:

Starting at the left centre front, pin in place the bottom edge of the seam binding tape at 9 ½"(24.1 cm) distance from the cast on edge of the WS left front panel. Use a running stitch to secure the bottom of the tape, work to 4 ½" (11.4 cm) from the left front panel side edge.

Fold this 4 ½" (11.4 cm) back, then measure 4 ½" (11.4 cm) from the back side, travel the seam binding across from front panel to the back placing seam binding at this measurement, and ensuring placement is 9 ½" (24.1 cm) from the

back cast on edge. Sew in place. Continue to work across the back until 4 ½" (11.4 cm) from the right side, fold this back, measure 4 ½" (11.4 cm) on right side panel. At this point, again travel across from back panel to front placing the seam binding, sewing it in place until you reach right centre front. Complete the casing by sewing the top of the binding tape with a running stitch.

Elastic in casing Using a safety pin, secure the elastic end and begin threading it through the created casing of the left front, across to the back, through back casing and across to right front. Adjust elastic to gather at the waist as desired. Secure elastic to binding tape at centre fronts and open sides.

I-cord ties With remaining yarn, create 2 -3 st 13" (33 cm) i-cords to be used as front ties for the kimono. Place a knot at the bottom of each i-cord. Sew the edge with no knot to the centre fronts at the seam binding.

Lace Charts

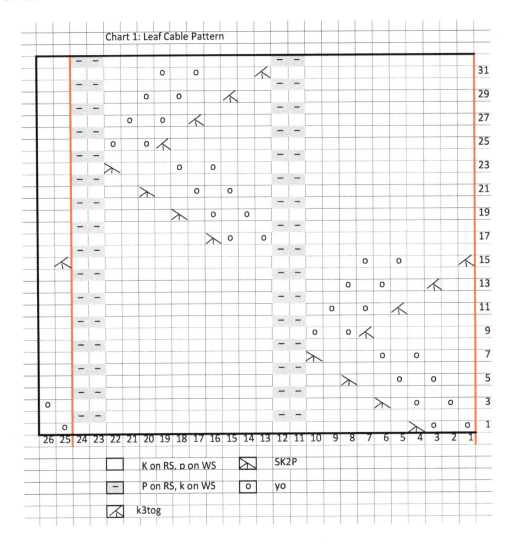

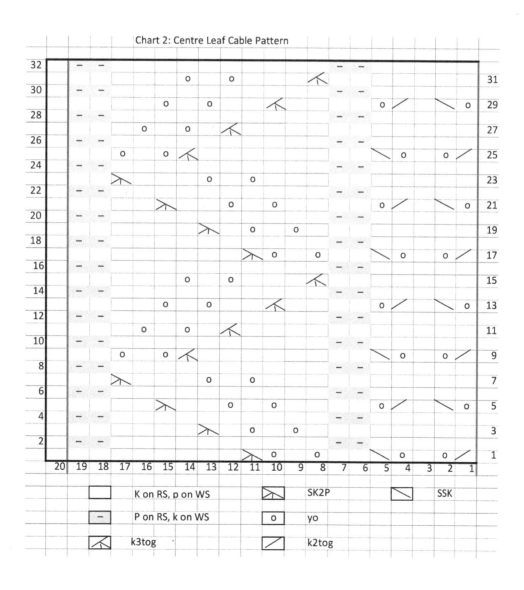

Chart 2: Centre Leaf Cable Pattern

NATURE'S KNIT-CH BOOK OF SINGLETS AND LIGHT COVERS — 107

Schematic

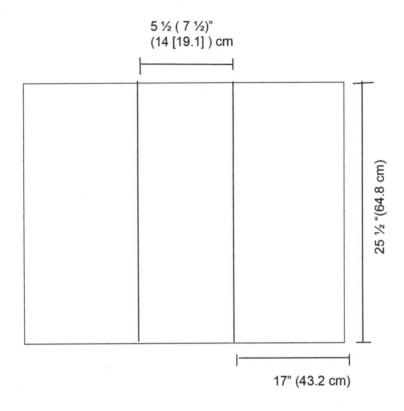

5 ½ (7 ½)"
(14 [19.1]) cm

25 ½ "(64.8 cm)

17" (43.2 cm)

LEAF

Colour, Colour, Colour! Seems odd that I would call this project Leaf, yet the leaf lace motif set against a garter stitch background is so feminine. The single ply wool from Custom Woolen Mills is my first foray with using a 1ply yarn and certainly won't be my last. I have to say that it was lovely to work with. This cover was knit bottom up incorporating the buttonband and using a circular needle to accommodate the large number of stitches. I liked the scalloping from the lace-garter combination, so no trim was required. I added some figure-flattering A-line shaping to the short sleeved cardi with vintage buttons accents.

Challenge Level	INTERMEDIATE
Finished Bust Size	S (M, L, XL, 2X, 3X) Bust 39 (42, 45, 48 ½, 55, 58 ½)" (99 [106.7, 114.3, 123.2, 139.7, 148.6]) cm
Yarn	2 (2, 3, 3, 3, 4) – 1ply mule spinner, 100% wool, 395/432yds 112g, Custom Woolen Mills, Carstairs, AB, CANADA.
Needles & Notions	3 ¼mm (3 US) 29" (73.7 cm) and 24" (60 cm) circular needles; stitch holders; 7 – 5/8" (1.6 cm) buttons
Gauge	23sts and 33 rows in 4" (10 cm) using 3 ¼mm needles and Chart #1 Garter Leaf Lace Pattern.
Care Instructions	Hand wash with a wool wash product. Lie flat to air dry.

INSTRUCTIONS

Body

Using long tail cast on method and size 3 ¼mm (3 US) circular needles, cast on 238 (257, 276, 295, 333, 352) sts. Note: 2 selvage stitches are included; on every row slip the first stitch and knit the last stitch. Knit the next row.

Next RS row: Establish pattern as per chart. Note: The pattern is symmetrical about the centre front garter bands. Work in pattern until 1" (2.5 cm) is completed from cast on edge before staring the A-line shaping.

Over the next 5" (12.7 cm) at 1" (2.5 cm) intervals complete the following:

Complete 3 Garter-lace repeats, on the next garter section, ssk, K4, k2tog (-2 sts), complete lace section. Reduce 2 st on the next garter section as follows: K2tog, k4, ssk, complete lace section. Resume full patterns of the garter-lace repeat, then repeat this reduction for the right side of the work. Explanation: The 2 st reductions occur in the garter sections of the pattern. Continue to complete these 2 st reductions further reducing these garter sections. At 5" (12.7 cm) , you should have a lace pattern followed by 2 purl stitches, followed by a lace pattern, then 2 purl stitches and another lace pattern. 222 (241, 260, 279, 317, 336) sts.

At the same time, in the first garter band create a 3 st one row buttonhole when 2" (5.1 cm) has been completed from the cast on edge. Continue to incorporate a 3 st buttonhole every 2 ½" (6.4 cm) from the previous buttonhole while completing the body.

When work measures 13 ½ (14, 14, 14 ½, 15)" (34.3 [35.6, 35.6, 36.8, 38.1]) cm from cast on edge, separate fronts from the back as follows to work each section separately:

Working in established pattern, complete 55 (60, 65, 70, 79, 84) sts, place remaining stitches on a holder or another cable needle.

Right Front

Size S (M): Next row (WS): Reduce 3 (5) sts at armhole edge. Continue to reduce 1 st every knit row until work measures 5 (5 ½)" (12.7 [14]) cm from first armhole cast off before shaping the neck edge. At the same time, continue to incorporate buttonholes as required.

Size L-3X: Reduce 5 (6, 6, 6) sts, then 2 (4, 5, 6) sts at armhole edge. Continue to reduce 1 st every knit row until work measures 6 (6 ½, 7, 7 ½)" (15.2 [16.5, 17.8, 19.1]) cm before shaping neck edge.

Neck edge shaping S1, k8, place these buttonband stitches onto a holder. At neck edge, reduce 4 sts, then 3 sts, then 2 sts, then 1 st. Continue to decrease 1 st at neck edge and continue to decrease at armhole edge every alternate row until armhole measures 8 ½ (9, 9 ½, 10, 10 ½, 11)" (21.6 [22.9, 24.1, 25.4, 26.7, 28]) cm. Cast off remaining stitches.

Back

Place 112 (121, 130, 139, 159, 168) sts onto the working needles from the holder. Attach a new yarn and over the next 2 rows cast off 3 (5, 5, 6, 6, 6) sts then 0(0, 2, 4, 5, 6) sts. Continue reducing 1 st each end every alternate row until armhole measures 8 ½ (9, 9 ½, 10, 10 ½, 11)" (21.6 [22.9, 24.1, 25.4, 26.7, 28]) cm from first armhole cast off. Back neck measures 6 ¼ (7 ½, 7 ½, 9 ½, 10, 10)" (15.9 [19.1, 19.1, 24.1, 25.4, 25.4]) cm. Cast off.

Left Front

Place remaining stitches 55 (60, 65, 70, 79, 84) sts onto working needles and complete shaping as follows:

Sizes S (M) next row (WS): Reduce 3 (5) sts at armhole edge. Continue to reduce 1 st every knit row until work measures 5 (5 ½)" (12.7 [14]) cm from first armhole cast off before shaping the neck edge.

Size L-3X: Reduce 5 (6, 6, 6) sts, then 2 (4, 5, 6) sts at armhole edge. Continue to reduce 1 st every knit row until work measures 6 (6 ½, 7, 7 ½)" (15.2 [16.5, 17.8, 19.1]) cm before shaping neck edge.

Neck edge shaping S1, k8, place these button band stitches onto a holder. At neck edge, reduce 4 sts, then 3 sts, then 2 sts, then 1 st. Continue to decrease 1 st at neck edge and continue to decrease at armhole edge every alternate row until armhole measures 8 ½ (9, 9 ½, 10, 10 ½, 11)" (21.6 [22.9, 24.1, 25.4, 26.7, 28]) cm. Cast off remaining stitches.

Sleeves

Using long tail cast on method and size 3 ¼mm (3 US) circular needles, cast on 82 (88, 90, 97, 99, 105) sts. Knit next row. Establish the pattern as follows:

Row (WS): s1, K2 (5, 6, 0, 1, 4) sts complete lace pattern repeats ending with k3 (6, 7, 1, 2, 5) sts. Continue to work in pattern and increase 1 st each end of sleeve every 8th (8, 6, 6, 6, 6) row until work measures 3 (3, 4, 4, 5, 6)" (7.6 [7.6, 10.2, 10.2, 12.7, 15.2]) cm from the cast on edge before completing armhole and cap shaping. 88 (94, 100, 107, 113, 121) sts.

Armhole and cap shaping For Size S (M): Over the next two rows, cast off 3 (5) sts. For Size L-3X: Over the next 4 rows cast off 5 (6, 6, 6) sts, then 2 (4, 5, 6) sts. Continue decreasing 1 st each end of every alternate row until armhole measures 8 ½ (9, 9 ½, 10, 10 ½, 11)" (21.6 [22.9, 24.1, 25.4, 26.7, 28]) cm with approximately 2" (5.1 cm) width remaining 15 (14, 11, 12, 12, 12) sts. Cast off.

Finishing

Sew sleeves to body. Weave in ends.

Garter neck band With RS facing and 24" (60 cm) circular needle, knit the stitches from the buttonholed button band, pick up stitches along the left front, shoulder of the sleeve, back, right shoulder, pick up stitches along left front and knit the stitches from the right garter band. Complete 3 rows of garter stitch (knit each row). Next Row: At curvature of left front *ssk, k5, repeat from * 3 times more. Note: This should take you across the sleeve to attachment with the back, work even with no decreases until reaching the attachment of the back to the right sleeve, *k2tog, k5; repeat from * 3 time more, knit to end. Cast off using suspended bind off technique.

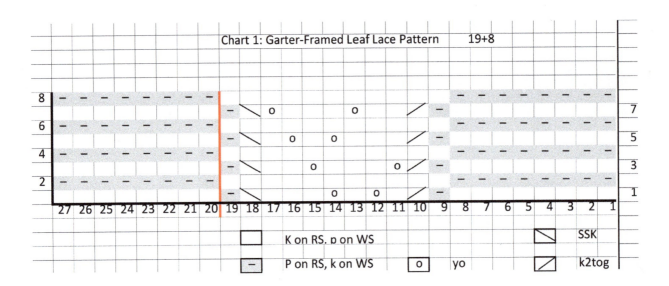

Schematic

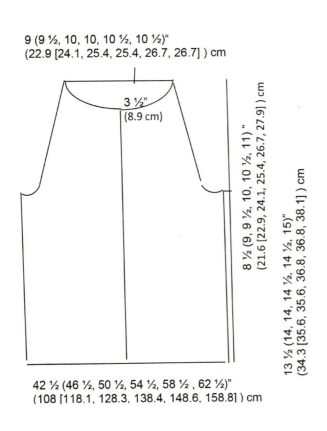

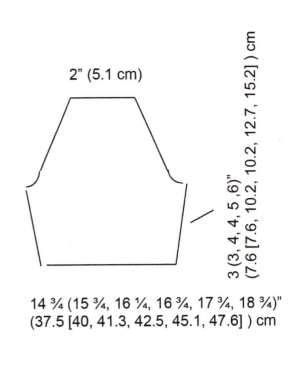

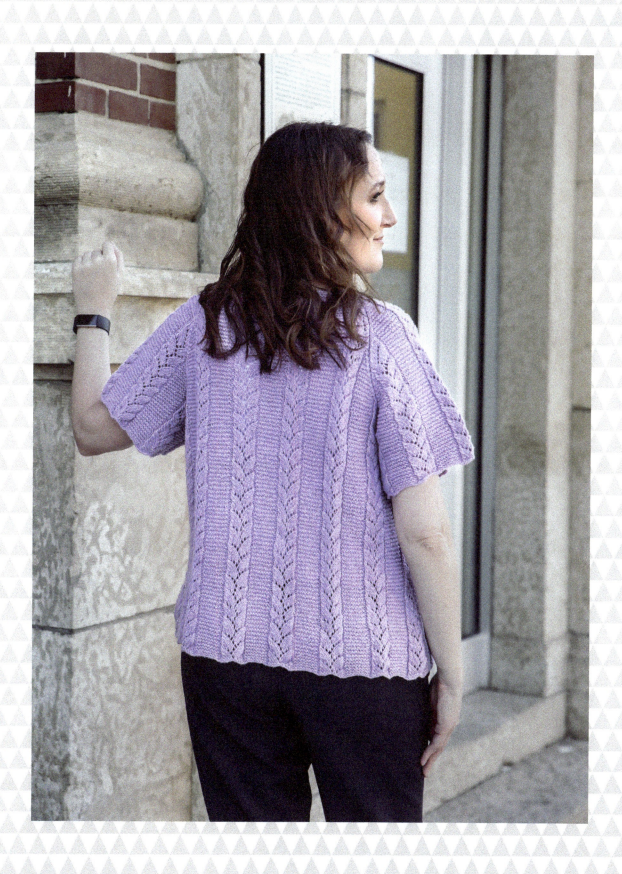

Cozy Cabled Cardi

Here is a cardi for those breezy days of summer. Stay warm in this lovely cardi designed in 100% wool (cool in summer, warm in winter). This design does not have pockets; however, you can choose to add them 3 ways – a slit pocket on the front, patch pocket on the front or my favorite a hidden pocket on the inside. Instructions are provided for all 3 types.

Challenge Level	INTERMEDIATE
Finished Bust Size	S (M, L, XL, 2X, 3X) Bust: 37 (41, 45, 49, 55, 57)" (94 [104.1, 114.3, 124.5, 139.7, 144.8]) cm
Yarn	6 (7, 8, 9, 10, 11) – 100% Canadian wool, 112g, 216yd 2ply mule spinner yarns, Custom Woolen Mills, Carstairs, AB, CANADA
Needles & Notions	4.0mm (6 US) straight and 24" (60 cm) circular needles, 7-¾" (1.9 cm) buttons, cable needle, stitch holder.
Gauge	26 sts and 32 rows in 4" (10 cm) using 4.0mm needles and cable pattern.
Care Instructions	Hand wash with a gentle wool wash product. Lie flat, block and air dry.

Cable Pattern (multiple of 7+3 and 2 selvage)

Row 1(RS): S1, p3, *k4, p3; repeat from *, end with k1.

Row 2: S1, *k3, p4; repeat from *, end k4.

Row 3 (cable cross): S1, p3, *2/2RC, p3; repeat from *, end with k1.

Rows 4: Repeat row 2.

Complete Rows 1-4 for pattern.

2/2 RC – S2 onto cable needle, hold to the back, k2; k2 from cable needle.

INSTRUCTIONS

Left Front

Using long tail cast on method and size 4.0mm (6 US) straight needles, cast on 61 (68, 75, 82, 89, 96) sts. Note: 2 selvage stitches are included; on every row slip the first stitch and knit the

last stitch of every row. Next row (WS): Knit.

Establish cable pattern (see Cable Pattern or Chart 1). Note: If you are considering adding slash pockets refer to the Pocket Options section. Work until piece measures 13 ½ (14, 14 ½, 15, 15 ½, 16)" (34.3 [35.6, 36.8, 38.1, 39.4, 40.6]) cm from cast on edge before shaping armhole.

Armhole shaping For Size S (M): Cast off 4 sts, then 3 sts, then 2 sts, then 1 st 3 (5) times at armhole edge. 12 (14) sts decreased.

For Size L-3X: Cast off 4 sts, then 3 sts, then 2 sts, then 1 st 1 (3, 5, 7) times at armhole edge. 15 (17, 19, 21) sts decreased.

When work measures 4 ½ (5, 5 ½, 6, 6 ½, 7)" (11.4 [12.7, 14, 15.2, 16.5, 17.8]) cm from start of armhole shaping complete neck shaping.

Neck shaping At the beginning of the next several rows cast off 5 sts, 4 sts, 3 sts, 2 sts. Continue to decrease 1 st every other row at neck edge. Work until armhole measures 8 ½ (9, 9 ½, 10, 10 ½, 11)" (21.6 [22.9, 24.1, 25.4, 26.7, 27.9]) cm from beginning of armhole shaping. Cast off remaining 21 (24, 28, 31, 34, 37) sts.

Right Front

Complete as directed for left front reversing all shaping.

Back

With 4.0 mm (6 US) needles cast on 117 (131, 145, 159, 173, 180) sts. Knit next row. Establish cable pattern. Work until piece measures 13 ½ (14, 14 ½, 15, 15 ½, 16)" (34.3 [35.6, 36.8, 38.1, 39.4, 40.6]) cm from cast on edge before shaping armhole.

Armhole shaping For Size S (M): At the start of the next several rows cast off 4 sts, then 3 sts, then 2 sts, then 1 st 3 (5) times at armhole edge. 24 (28) sts decreased.

For Size L-3X: At the start of the next several rows cast off 4 sts, then 3 sts, then 2 sts, then 1 st 1 (3, 5, 7) times at armhole edge. 30 (34, 38, 42) sts decreased.

Work without decreases until the armhole measures 6 ½ (7, 7 ½, 8, 8 ½, 9)" (16.6 [17.8, 19.1, 20.3, 21.6, 22.9]) cm from start of armhole shaping before completing neck shaping.

Neck shaping Work 27 (30, 34, 37, 40, 43) sts and place onto a holder. Cast off the centre 39 (42, 45, 48, 51, 54) sts, complete the row.

With WS facing you, place stitches from holder back onto the needles, attach yarn and complete neck shaping for the right side.

Over the next several rows at the neck edge cast off 3 sts, then 2 sts, then 1 st.

Work until armhole measures 8 ½ (9, 9 ½, 10, 10 ½, 11)" (21.6 [22.9, 24.1, 25.4, 26.7, 27.9]) cm from

beginning of armhole shaping. Cast off remaining 21 (24, 28, 31, 34, 37) sts.

Sleeves

Cast on 57 (57, 68, 68, 70, 75) sts. Next 3 rows: Knit. Establish p3, k4 pattern without completing the cable cross and work until sleeve measures 3" (7.6 cm) from cast on edge. Change to cable pattern completing 4" (10.2 cm) of this pattern. Start to increase each end of every 6th row and work until sleeve measures 16 (16 ½, 17, 17 ½, 18, 18 ½)" (40.6 [41.9, 43.2, 44.5, 45.7, 47]) cm from cast on edge before completing armhole and cap shaping.

Armhole and cap shaping For Size S(M): At the start of the next several rows cast off 4 sts, then 3 sts, then 2 sts, then 1 st 3 (5) times at armhole edge. 24 (28) sts decreased.

For Size L-3X: At the start of the next several rows cast off 4 sts, then 3 sts, then 2 sts, then 1 st 1 (3, 5, 7) times at armhole edge. 30 (34, 38, 42) sts decreased.

Continue to decrease 1 st each end of every knit row for all sizes until work measures 5 ¾ (6, 6 ⅓, 6 ⅔, 7, 7 ⅓)" (14.6 [15.2, 16.1, 17, 17.8, 18.6]) cm from beginning of armhole shaping before shaping the cap.

Over the next several rows, cast off 2 sts at the start of the row 3 times, then 3 sts at the start of the row twice. Cast off remaining stitches.

Complete the other sleeve.

Finishing

Sew backs to fronts at shoulders. Sew in sleeves and sides.

Button bands

Left side With RS facing, pick up stitches evenly along centre front edge such that ½ of the stitch is visible on the front side of the work creating an obvious vertical line. Next row establish pattern of k4, p3. As you create the last knit stitch of the k4, increase f&b in this stitch counting the increase as one of the purl stitches in pattern. Work 7 rows in pattern, then cast off loosely using suspended bind off technique.

Complete buttonhole band incorporating 7 3 st buttonholes as follows:

Right side With RS facing, pick up stitches evenly along centre front edge such that ½ of the stitch is visible on the front side of the work creating an obvious vertical line. Next row establish pattern of k4, p3 and as you create the last knit stitch of the k4, increase f&b in this stitch counting the increase as one of the purl stitches in pattern. Work 3 rows in pattern, then on the next row create 7-3 st one row buttonholes approximately 2" (5.1cm) apart. Complete another 2 full rows of pattern. Cast off next row using suspended bind off technique.

Collar

With right side facing and 4.0mm (6 US) circular needle, pick up stitches evenly from left front, back and right front. Establish the k4, p3 pattern. Work in pattern for a further 2 rows. Decrease row: K4, *p2, p2tog, k3; repeat from * to end of row. Without further decrease complete 3 more rows of pattern then cast off using suspended bind off method.

Weave in ends. Sew on buttons.

Pocket Options

Slash Pockets Slash pockets are strategically place at 1/3 distance from the side of the front panel (2/3 distance from the centre front edge). Incorporate the pocket approximately 1" (2.5 cm)from any ribbing e.g., 1" (2.5 cm) from a 2 ½-3" (6.4-7.6 cm) ribbing. In the case of this sweater, at 4" (10.2 cm) from the cast on edge.

Working on a left front panel RS row, knit (or pattern) across to 3 sts before the 2/3 mark. Cast off the next 3 sts, work to end. Next row: Purl to 1 st before cast off, knit the stitch. Attach another yarn after the 3st gap and work to end. Continue to build the slash pocket length to approximately 5 ½ or 6 " (14 or 15.2 cm) before joining the two pieces back together. To join; work to gap, cable cast on 3 sts, work to end. Note: The 3 sts allows for a nice pocket finish.

Complete the same slash pocket working on the right-side panel, knit to 3 sts before the 1/3 mark to start the slash pocket.

Create linings These can be worked separately (cast on to match the height of your slash pocket) or you can pick up stitches along the open edge of the pocket. Work for 1" (2.5 cm) without increase. To create depth to the pocket, increase 1" (2.5 cm) using cable cast on at the start of the next row. Continue in stockinette until work measures 5" (12.7 cm) from cast on edge. Cast off using the suspended bind off method. Block and stitch pocket lining to pocket opening.

Finish front face of pocket With RS facing, working vertically, pick up 1 st before the slash pocket edge, all stitches along the edge and 1 st after the slash pocket edge. Work a rib pattern or garter stitch edge for 3 rows. Cast off. Secure top and bottom edges of the pockets to the front panels.

Design Note: When you have a highly patterned sweater, you want to be clever in the placement of a pocket so that the design is not disrupted. You can choose to place the pocket in between cables or opt for a patch pocket design placed on top of the front panel or hide a pocket inside the sweater.

Patch Pockets A typical patch pocket is 4 ½ -5" (11.4-12.7 cm) wide and 5 ½-6" (14-15.2 cm) in length. The size is really up to you. Choose to mirror the current pattern where you want to place the pockets. Make 2. Placement of the pocket is centered on the front panel. I sew mine in place with a 3 ply embroidery floss that closely matches the yarn.

Hidden Pocket The goal with the hidden pocket is to be as flat as possible so you don't add additional bulk to the design. I work it up in stockinette stitch as follows:

For a 7" (17.8 cm) wide pocket:

Cast on required number of stitches based on your gauge. Work for 5" (12.7 cm) in stockinette stitch. Next row: Work 1" (2.5 cm), create a one-row buttonhole that is 5" (12.7 cm) wide, work to end of row. Continue to complete 1" (2.5 cm) before casting off. Weave in ends. Block. Sew to the inside right or left front panel of the sweater. The one row buttonhole works well as a pocket opening and does not need extra finishing.

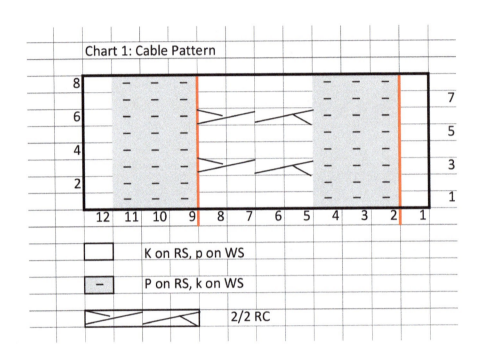

Schematic

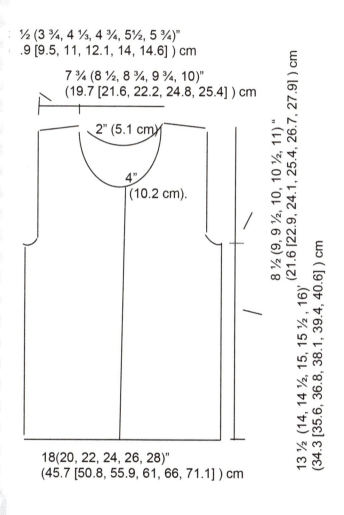
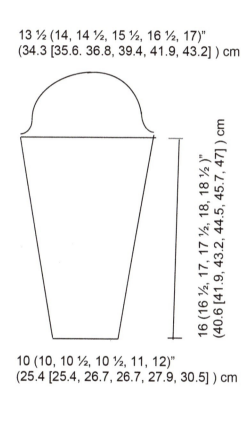

NATURE'S KNIT-CH BOOK OF SINGLETS AND LIGHT COVERS — 123

Round We Go Cardi

Sometimes all it takes to inspire a design is a button! This cardi was created with a big black button in mind. The button was gifted to me by a fellow member of the High River Handicrafts Guild. I thought a nice circular collar band would showcase it nicely. This cardi is knit from the left sleeve, fronts and backs are added on, pockets are created on the left front. The right front is then knit and connected to the back and then finally knit to create the right sleeve. Hence Round We Go. The bottom edge of the cardi is a garter band increased as you go by short rows so it doesn't pull in too much. 2 long cable needles are required for this knit to hold the large number of stitches.

Challenge Level	INTERMEDIATE
Finished Bust Size	S (M, L, XL, 2X, 3X)
	Bust: 38 (42, 46, 50, 54, 58)" (96.5 [106.7, 116.8, 127, 137.2, 147.3]) cm
Yarn	3 (3, 4, 4, 4, 5) – 100% Canadian wool, 112g, 216yd 2ply mule spinner yarns, Custom Woolen Mills, Carstairs, AB, CANADA
Needles & Notions	5.0mm (8 US) 2 – 36" circular needles; 24 " circular; 1– 1" button, stitch holder.
Gauge	16 sts and 22 rows in 4" (10 cm) using 5.0mm needles and stockinette.
Care Instructions	Hand wash with a gentle wool wash product. Lie flat, block and air dry.

INSTRUCTIONS

Left Sleeve

Using long tail cast on method and size 5.0mm (8 US) circular needles, cast on 58 (62, 66, 70, 74, 78) sts. Note: 2 selvage stitches are included; on every row slip the first stitch and knit the last stitch.

Create 1" (2.5 cm) of garter stitch before changing to stockinette stitch. Work until sleeve measures 5 ½" (14 cm) from cast on edge before shaping armhole.

Armhole shaping

Begin increasing 1 st each end of every other row until 2 ½" (6.4 cm) has been created on both sides of the sleeve (20 sts increased) 78 (82, 86, 90, 94, 98) sts.

Back and fronts At the beginning of the next row cable cast on loosely 50 (52, 56, 60, 64, 68) sts and knit this row 128 (134, 142, 150, 158, 166) sts. Next row increase using a purlwise cable cast on into the first stitch, cast on another 50 (52, 56, 60, 64, 68) sts. Knit the row placing a marker after 20 sts and a marker when 20 sts remain before finishing the row. Note: This will form the garter bands at the bottom front and back of the cardi 178 (184, 198, 210, 222, 234) sts. Establish garter (knit every row) for the 20 sts, change to stockinette and work to marker, slip marker, create another garter edge of 20 sts. Work in this manner until work is 2" (5.1 cm) from cast on edge of front and back.

Garter band short row shaping: On the next row and every 2" (5.1 cm) as you knit the front and back width, increase the garter band as follows:

K19 sts, bring yarn to front, slip stitch purlwise before marker, place yarn in back, slip the wrapped stitch back onto left needle, turn the work. Knit to end of row. Complete the same shaping for the other side.

Work until 2 ¼ (2 ¾, 3, 3 ½, 4, 4 ½)" (5.7 [7, 7.6, 8.9, 10.2, 11.4]) cm has been completed from cast on edge before shaping neck edge. On the RS row work to 2 sts before midpoint 87 (90, 97, 103, 109, 115), cast off 4 sts, knit to end. This separates the back and front at the left neck edge. You can now work the fronts and backs separately or if you prefer or attach another ball of yarn to complete the back at the same time. Remember to increase your garter section every 2" (5.1 cm) as you work across.

Left front with pocket

Continue working left front as follows: At neck edge every other row, decrease 1 st (s1, ssk) work to garter, complete garter to end of row. When 2 ¼ (2 ¾, 3, 3 ½, 4, 4 ½)" (5.7 [7, 7.6, 8.9, 10.2, 11.4]) cm has been created on the front panel, create pocket opening as follows: On the next knit row, work garter section 19 sts then knit into the front and back (f&b) of the next stitch (1 st increase). Place these 21 sts onto a holder.

In the next stitch of the front body, cable cast on 15 sts for the pocket facing. Work these stitches along with the body in stockinette, continuing to reduce 1 st at neck edge every other row. Work until width of pocket lining is 5" (12.7 cm). Cast off the 15 sts for pocket facing on the next row, knit to end.

Garter Pocket Place the 21 sts from holder onto 5.0mm (8 US) needles, s1, knit to last stitch, k1. Note: This extra stitch is a selvage stitch which creates the finish to the top opening of the pocket. Continue in garter until 5" (12.7 cm) from the beginning in preparation for joining to the front body.

Next RS row: Work down from neck edge to bottom edge, knit the last stitch of the body together with the slipped stitch of the garter section to rejoin, complete garter section. Work all stitches now for 2" (5.1 cm) measured from pocket joining. Work until width of front measured in stockinette is 9 ½ (10 ½, 11 ½, 12 ½, 13 ½, 14 ½)" (24.1 [26.7, 29.2, 31.8, 34.3, 36.8]) cm. Cast off remaining 63 (65, 72, 74 ,79, 83) sts.

Back

With 5.0 mm (8 US) needles, join another ball of yarn, s1, k2tog at neck edge and complete the row. Continue to build the width of the back, reducing 1 st at neck edge every other row and increasing the garter section (short row shaping) until work measures 9 ½ (10 ½, 11 ½, 12 ½, 13 ½, 14 ½)" (24.1 [26.7, 29.2, 31.8, 34.3, 36.8]) cm from back cast on edge. At this point the neck edge is increased by 1 st every other row as you work across the right side back. Work until width of back is 16 ¾ (18 ¼, 20, 21 ½, 23, 24 ½)" (42.5 [46.4, 50.8, 54.6, 58.4, 62.2]) cm to prepare to join right front.

Right front with pocket

Cast on 63 (65, 72, 74 ,79, 83) sts. Establish pattern – 1 st increase at neck edge and 20 sts garter section at the bottom. Continue building the right front width until 2 ¼ (2 ¾, 3 ½, 4, 4 ½, 5)" (5.7 [7, 8.9, 10.2, 11.4, 12.7]) cm is complete measured from cast on edge. Complete pocket as described for left pocket opening. Continue to work the pocket lining and right front body for 5" (12.7 cm) before rejoining the garter band to complete the pocket.

Join Back and Right Front Once the pocket is complete, the right front is joined to the back at the shoulders. Work to shoulder (either back or front), cast on 4 sts, join back or front. Work even following all established patterns until back width measures 19 (21, 23, 25, 27, 29)" (48.3 [53.3, 58.4, 63.5, 68.9, and front measures 9 ½ (10 ½, 11 ½, 12 ½, 13 ½, 14 ½)" (24.1 [26.7, 29.2, 31.8, 34.3, 36.8]) cm from right front cast on edge. Next two rows: Cast off 50 (52, 56, 60, 64, 68) sts using the suspended bind off method, knit to end.

Armhole shaping On the next several rows, reduce 1 st at each end of every alternate row until 58 (62, 66, 70, 74, 78) sts remain.

Right Sleeve

Work without decrease for 4 ½" (11.4 cm). Change to garter stitch and complete 1" (2.5 cm). Cast off stitches using suspended bind off method.

Finishing

Weave in ends. Sew backs to fronts at side seams and sleeves. Sew pocket linings to fronts.

Centre front bands With RS facing, pick up stitches evenly along centre front edge such that ½ of the stitch is visible on the front side of the work creating an obvious vertical line. Next row knit to establish garter pattern for 3 rows. Cast off.

Collar With right side facing and 5.0mm (8 US) 24" (60 cm) circular needle, pick up stitches evenly from left front, place shoulder marker, pick up shoulder stitches, place shoulder marker, pick up back stitches, place shoulder marker, pick up right shoulder stitches, place marker and pick up right front increasing 1 st for every 4 sts (knit 3, k1 f&b). Knit the next row. Begin decreases to shape the collar as follows:

Knit to 2 sts before marker, k2tog, slip marker, knit across shoulder, slip next marker, ssk, knit across the back to 2 sts before the marker, k2tog, slip the marker, knit across shoulder to next marker, slip marker, ssk, knit remaining stitches. Next row: Knit. Complete these 2 rows twice more.

Next Row: In addition to reducing at the markers, knit 7, k2tog on the front neck edges and back neck edge. Next row knit. Continue decreasing at the shoulder edge only completing 4 more rows.

When work measures 2" (5.1 cm) from start of collar create a one-row buttonhole to accommodate the button, then *knit 5, k2tog; repeat from * maintaining the decrease of 1 st before and after shoulder markers. Continue decreasing at the shoulder edge only for 4 more rows.

Work without any decreases for 6 rows before casting off using the suspended bind off method. Collar should measure 3 ½" (8.9 cm) from collar cast on.

Weave in ends. Sew on buttons.

Schematic

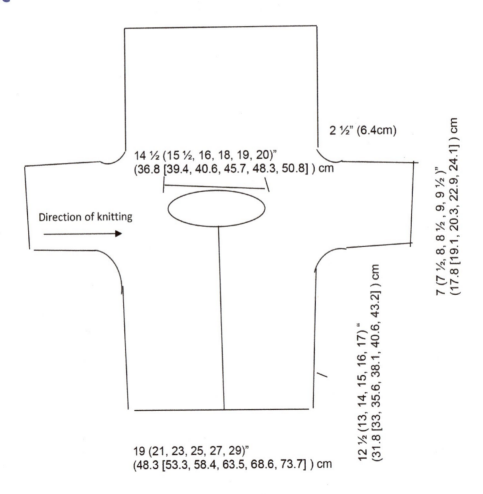

Yarn Sources

The following is a list of yarns used in this book. I am proud to say that most are sourced in Canada from farms (animal to skein).

1. Cestari Sheep and Wool Company, 2570 Little Calf Pasture Hwy. Swoop, VA 24472 (540)997-1212 website: cestarisheep.com

2. Custom Woolen Mills, 30453 Range Road 27-2, Carstairs, AB T0M 0N0. (403)337-2221 website: customwoolenmills.com

3. Heart West Haven, Priddis, AB T0L 1K0

4. Hemp for Knitting, 320 Vernon St., Suite 3B, Nelson, BC V1L 4E4. (250) 352-6985. Website: lanaknits.com

5. Homespun Haven, 4165 Round Prairie Road, Armstrong, BC V0E 1B4 (604) 546-3224 email: handspun@telus.net

6. John Bead Corporation Limited. 20 Bertrand Ave, Scarborough, ON M1K 2P4 website: johnbead.com

7. Morrison Creek Farm and Fibre, 4254 Miromar Rd, Courtenay, BC V9N 9N1 (250)334-4527

8. Mountain Sunset Angoras, Box 66, Pincher Creek, AB T0K 1W0 (403)627-4240 csheard@jrtwave.com

9. Sarah Elizabeth Fibre Works Studio and Shop 2002 Washington St., Rossland, BC. V0G 1Y0 website: sarahelizabethfibreworks.ca

10. Sunnyview Alpacas, Box 489 Clavet, SK, S0K 0Y0 (306)374-2636. Website: sunnyviewalpacas.com

11. Twisted Sisters & Company Fibre Mill, 50122 Range Road 225, Leduc County, AB T0B 3M3
(780)918-0365 website: twistedsistersmill.com

12. Wild Geese Fibres, ravelry.com/yarn/brands/wild-geese-fibres

Knitting Techniques

Here is a collection of my favorite knitting techniques. I have used these techniques throughout this book. Over the years, I have tried to explore different techniques to improve or enhance my knitting skills. I gravitate to these techniques because they deliver consistent results for me. Oh, and once you have learned the one-row buttonhole, you will never go back!

Shoulder Seam Stitch

The key to the shoulder seam stitch is getting the first two stitches aligned correctly then duplicating them as you sew the shoulders together. I always start at the neckline and work towards the armhole edge. Instructions are as follows:

1. Place shoulder seams flat so that the front panel of the work matches the back panel.

2. Create the figure 8. Secure a length of yarn with a darning needle to the WS front edge neckline. Bring the yarn through to the front panel at the neckline cast off edge, and then underneath and through to the front of the back panel neckline cast off edge. Bring the yarn back to the front panel again through to the front the work at the neckline cast off edge. Secure the figure 8 created. This ensures alignment of both knitting pieces at the neck edge.

3. Pick up the "V". Insert your darning needle with yarn into and around the first full stitch, the "V" above the cast off edge on the back panel.

4. Pick up the corresponding "A" (or upside-down "V") on the front panel. An explanation: The knit stitch has two legs visually (left and right) that form each stitch. In the shoulder seam stitch, we create a stitch with our yarn around the first stitch "the V" on the back panel, then we want to move to the next stitch on the front panel to get ready to pick up the next "V" on the back panel and so on, so with our darning needle we go down through the left leg of the stitch and up through the right leg of the next stitch on the front panel. This visually looks like we are picking up an upside-down V.

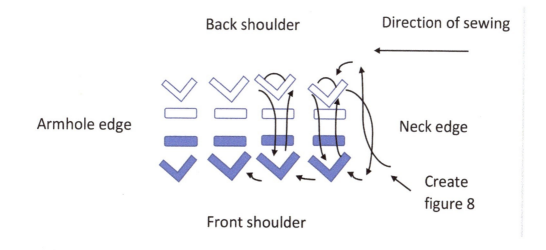

5. Repeat this sequence, by returning to the back panel and picking up the next full stitch "V". Secure yarn when complete.

Long Tail Cast On

I find this method never fails to give me a nice edge that has enough stretch (better than cable cast on) but is not sloppy. The key to long tail cast on is to measure 1" for every stitch you intend to put on the needle. This tip works great for thick yarns e.g., bulky, aran weights but you can reduce this when you are working with fingering (try ½" / stitch) or worsted weights (try ¾" / stitch). Once you do this a couple of times, you will know what multiplier e.g., ½, ¾ to use so you don't end up with a big long tail. Also, I typically will purl/knit the next row making it the wrong side (WS) of my work.

Creating the long tail cast on is as follows:

1. Measure your yarn to correspond to the number of stitches you want on the needle.

2. Create a backwards loop, place this loop on the right hand needle such that the measured portion of yarn is in front of you, yarn from the ball is in the back.

3. With your left hand, place your index finger and thumb between the two yarns on the needle. This creates a triangle visually – needle with yarn at the top, thumb in front and index finger in back.

4. Grasp the two yarns hanging down with your other fingers capturing them against your palm.

5. Flip your thumb and index fingers counter-clockwise from their horizontal placement to a vertical position.

6. Creating the stitch. With right needle, proceed to pick up yarn in front of the thumb from front to back (as if to knit), then pick up yarn on the index finger from back to front (as if to purl) returning through the loop created on the thumb.

7. Secure the created stitch on the right needle.

Repeat Steps 6 & 7 until the desired number of stitches are on the right needle. I recommend knitting or purling the first stitch on the next row to secure the cast on.

Suspended Bind Off

Such an awesome bind off! Very similar to our standard bind off technique, but this technique ensures the cast off edge is not too tight. Instructions are as follows:

1. As with standard binding off, work to create two stitches on the right needle.

2. With the left needle, pick up the first stitch on the right needle and proceed to place it over the second stitch on the needle. Do not drop the stitch. With the right needle, insert it knitwise into the next stitch on the left needle, create the stitch to move onto the right needle. As the stitch is moved to the right needle, the held stitch on the left needle is allowed to drop. Understanding why this works: By holding the stitch out from the neck of the second stitch we prevent the stitch from choking it (getting too tight). Note: You have to think ahead when you are switching between a purl cast off and knit cast off. Move the yarn to the desired position before suspending the stitch.

One Row Buttonhole

Once you learn this technique you will never go back to 2 row buttonholes. It takes a bit of practice and then you will fly along creating buttonholes. Note: The one row buttonhole can also be used to insert a pocket opening in the front of a garment! You will need to have your button size selected and I advise making a swatch with the buttonhole as you want the button to move with some tension through the buttonhole. Instructions are as follows:

1. Work to where you want to place your first buttonhole. At this point, place the yarn in front, slip the next stitch on the left needle purlwise, place the yarn in back. This will wrap the first stitch of the buttonhole.

2. Slip the next stitch from the left needle purlwise, insert the left needle into the wrapped stitch and bring it over the first stitch on the needle (1 stitch has been removed). Complete this step for the number of stitches required for the buttonhole e.g., 3 sts, 4 sts, etc. When complete, turn the work so the purl side of the work is facing you.

3. With yarn in front, insert the right needle between the last stitch on the left needle and second last stitch, purl cable cast on stitches to the left needle. Note: Be careful with the tension of your cable cast on, you want the stitch length to mirror the bottom edge of the buttonhole. Purl cable cast on until you have the number of stitches needed for the buttonhole and 1 extra stitch e.g., if you need a 3 st buttonhole, you will purl cable cast on 4 sts. Turn the work.

4. With the right needle, slip the next stitch on the left needle knitwise onto the right needle, insert the left needle into the second stitch on the right needle (last cable cast on stitch) and place it over the first stitch on the needles. This secures the last stitch of the buttonhole.

Beading and Knitting

There is something about those shiny little seed beads that add that extra sparkle to your knitting. I like to add beads as you will see in many of my projects. It makes them extra special.

The secret to beading is having a beading needle with an enlarged eye. The beading needle must be fine enough to fit through the bead including the additional yarn. Enlarging the eye can be done many ways – dental floss, fly line, or firewire (used in beading). The firewire is threaded through the eye to create a loop and tied off with an overhand knot. The yarn that you want to thread with beads is then threaded through this new loop with ease. Now you are ready to pick up your beads.

Acknowledgments

Many thanks to Jess and the team at Friesen Press for educating me on publishing and working with me on this journey.

Many thanks to Cara Rochford, Bijou Bee Photography and her team of Carol Thompson (model, makeup & fashion consultant), Nicola Laboucane (model), and Jessica Gabriel (model). All photos were shot at local locations in High River and Okotoks including Highwood Museum, Maggie's Diner, Wales Movie Theatre, Colossi's Coffee House, The Dining Car at High River Station, Evelyn's Diner, Beachwood Area, CIBC, Olive and Finch, Carlson's on Macleod, Mclaughlin Meadows Community Garden, The Noble Tea House, George Lane Park, Highwood Memorial Centre, St. Benedict's Anglican Church, Pixie Hollow, Rotary Park Gazebo, Hollyhock Lane and Crystal Shores Beach.

To my partner in life, Keith – Thank you for showing me so much of what nature has to offer with our trips out into the wilderness. Thank you for your love and support with this book endeavor.

Index

1 x 1 Twisted Rib Pattern, 17
    Attaching i-cords, 43
    Beaded fringe, 63
    Beaded loop neck edge, 23
    Beaded Rib Twist pattern, 26
    Beading and knitting, 100
    Braided cord, 56
    cable cast on, 33, 34
    casing with seam binding tape, 78
    changing skeins., 30
    Create button loops, 49
    dart shaping, 14
    eyelet border, 73
    garter band, 93

Gazebo Lace, 8
    Hidden Pocket, 90
    Horizontal back band, 10
    i-cord bind off, 43
    I-cord ties, 79
    jacquard patterning, 73
    k1, p1 ribbing pattern, 38
    knit cast on, 39, 62

Lace Pattern for Locks, 37
    Long Tail Cast On, 98
    long tail cast on method, 9, 14, 17, 18, 21, 22, 26, 29, 30, 33, 34, 38, 39, 41, 42, 46, 47, 48, 53, 58, 66, 71, 73, 75, 77, 78, 82, 84, 88, 93
    mattress stitch, 63
    one row buttonhole, 83
    One row buttonhole, 99
    one row buttonhole technique, 68
    Optional beading, 59
    Optional Beading, 48, 49
    Patch Pockets, 90

Perforated Stitch, 70
    Pocket Options, 90
    purl cable cast on, 34, 66
    raglan, 38

Rib Stitch Pattern, 62
    Shaped Hood, 55
    Shaping Row, 67
    Shoulder bands, 10
    Shoulder Seam Stitch, 98
    single chain stitch, 19
    single crochet edge, 23
    single ply wool, 82
    slash pockets, 88
    Slash Pockets, 90
    suri alpaca, 77
    Suspended bind off, 99
    suspended bind off method, 71, 74
    suspended bind off technique, 84
    swiss darning / overstitching, 75
    transition to light yarn, 47, 48
    Waist shaping, 38

CPSIA information can be obtained
at www.ICGtesting.com
Printed in the USA
LVHW081505120523
746842LV00007B/116